DISCI-PLESHIP PROJECT

LUCAS LEYS
DAVID NOBOA

DISCI-PLESHIP PROJECT

LUCAS LEYS
DAVID NOBOA

e625.com

DISCIPLESHIP PROJECT – JUNIOR HIGH MINISTRY
e625 - 2023
Dallas, Texas
e625 ©2023 by **Lucas Leys and David Noboa**

____

All Bible verses are from the New International Version (NIV) unless otherwise specified.

Translated by: Josiah Brown

Interior design and cover by JuanShimabukuroDesign

ALL RIGHTS RESERVED.

ISBN: 978-1-954149-53-3

PRINTED IN THE UNITED STATES OF AMERICA

CONTENTS

INTRO

Success is only a consequence of having developed discipline with perseverance.

Lucas Leys, *Stamina*

In the Bible we find the story of when Jesus, after his resurrection, had an encounter with two of his disciples while they were walking toward Emmaus, a city located 10 kilometers from Jerusalem. As we read in this story from Luke chapter 24, those who claimed to be his followers did not know, at that moment, who he was. Doesn't that statement intrigue you? How is it that those who recognized themselves as his followers could not recognize him? The answers can be many. Some illustrate Jesus hidden behind a cloak, others say that his glorified image was different from his human form previous to the crucifixion, or perhaps he had the ability to confuse people's eyes so that they did not recognize him. The truth is that they did not know who he was until the moment he broke the bread and only then could they recognize him.

Whatever the explanation, the story highlights a powerful truth: It is not enough to know who Jesus is. Jesus can walk with you without you being able to recognize him, and suddenly, poof! a great revelation comes into your life that makes you see clearly that Jesus has been walking and talking with you the whole time.

THAT IS THE TASK OF THE DISCIPLERS: WALK WITH SOMEONE SO THEY CAN CLEARLY SEE JESUS.

That is the task of disciplers: walk with someone so that they can clearly see Jesus; accompanying another who still cannot recognize him in certain aspects of their life. And that is the challenge of biblical discipleship: traveling with another person until they can recognize the Messiah, their inner blindfolds drop, and they experience the presence of God through the risen Christ.

WHAT DISCIPLESHIP IS NOT

On many occasions, the clearest way to define something is to list what it is not, and here is a list of what biblical discipleship is not

- **IT IS NOT A BIBLE CLASS.** Usually, these two expressions get confused with each other since they often go hand in hand, but they are not the same. Teaching the Bible is an indispensable part of discipleship and that is why this book contains lessons to teach. However, this book includes the word *project* because just teaching a Bible class is not the whole of discipleship.

- **IT IS NOT A MEMBERSHIP PROGRAM.** In some churches it is believed that discipleship is an initiation program for new believers. We want new believers to start being disciples of Jesus and it is great that there is a good program for those who are taking their first steps in faith. But discipleship does not end with baptism or with the completion of a course. It is not about attending a series of workshops. Although these can help a lot in the discipleship process, you will see that biblical knowledge and other types of learning do not necessarily result in greater spiritual maturity.

- **IT IS NOT A DOCTRINAL REFLECTION.** Discipleship is not limited to intellectual matters. Rather, it is a process of integral character development that involves, in addition to the brain, the spirit, emotions, will, and conduct. Theology classes could make us fall into the delusion that by learning certain doctrines, we will be good disciples. The doctrines, of course, are fundamental and there is doctrinal teaching in true biblical discipleship, but those doctrines must be put into action to have an effect. Knowing theology and doctrine does not make you a good disciple if it does not lead to a tangible practice. Consider, for example, the Pharisees, whom Jesus was confronting. They had a lot of knowledge, and they handled theology and doctrine perfectly, but their hearts were far from God.

GENUINE DISCIPLESHIP IS MORE LIKE BEING A MIRROR OF CHRIST THAN SIMPLY TEACHING ABOUT HIM.

- **IT IS NOT A LITURGY.** Although it is. It is true that discipleship has a lot to do with acquiring good habits and spiritual disciplines, these things should not become cold repetitions or rigid religious behavior. Each discipline acquired, each moment of collective worship, each act of community participation, prayer, and fasting, are tools for our hearts to be conquered by the heart of Jesus and not only for us to "do" what is right in the eyes of others.

One can know a lot about God and be far from him, and because of this, genuine discipleship is more like being a mirror of Christ than simply teaching about him.

The point is not to "show" who is more like Jesus but to be clear that the more I focus on willingly reflecting Christ, the better discipler I will be.

So, what is biblical discipleship? Putting together just one sentence that includes all that genuine discipleship means can be very daring. . . but we can try:

**CHRISTIAN DISCIPLESHIP IS A PROCESS OF ACCOMPANIMENT }
IN WHICH, THROUGH A PERSONAL RELATIONSHIP,
SOMEONE IS ABLE TO FACILITATE IN THE DISCIPLE THE VIRTUES
OF THE CHARACTER OF JESUS.**

THINK OF THESE TWO WORDS

- **PROCESS:** Discipleship is a progressive and patient process. It has to do with accompanying a person from one place to another, just as it happened with the travelers in Emmaus. As they walked, Jesus reminded them of things they had already heard and told them things they did not yet know. And they lived the "process" of that walk with such intensity that when they finally realized it was their Master, they remembered that their hearts burned while he spoke to them.

- **RELATIONSHIP:** Discipleship does not happen without accompaniment. Walking together with someone means "being there" for that person. It's not just about giving lessons or classes, and it needs to be more than just a weekly meeting. Discipleship goes beyond being together for church services or scheduled meetings. The best disciplers share other moments of life with their apprentices and that is why the lessons in this book will challenge you to move from the lesson into community. That's how Jesus did it. And that is how we will do it.

THE MORE I FOCUS ON VOLUNTARILY REFLECTING CHRIST, THE BETTER DISCIPLER I WILL BE.

The twelve disciples were not the only followers of Jesus, but they were the most intimate. Throughout the time that our Messiah walked among human beings, many were close to him and that is still true today. Do you remember the crowd eating freely of the loaves and fishes?

There may be many followers of Jesus, but not all who claim to follow him are truly his disciples.

The Bible says that the Word became flesh and dwelt among us. He lived with men proclaiming that the kingdom of heaven had drawn near. He died. He rose again. And just before leaving to return to the throne prepared for him, he left a great task: *Go and make disciples, teach them to observe all the things that I have told you.* Then it is said that more than 500 people witnessed the ascension of the Savior (1 Corinthians 15:6).

The great task of making disciples of all nations is being carried out with various nuances, and in initiating this project in our churches, the imperative question to answer is: How can we make better disciples of Jesus?

As you go through this book, you will be given 10 crucial premises about the different aspects that biblical discipleship represents. Beyond the transmission of knowledge, these premises are intended to help you in the transmission of a CUL-TURE. That is what Christ came to establish: the culture of the kingdom of heaven, the precise interpretation of what the Father had said since ancient times, the social exercise of a people, which we now call family, and the characteristics that this family must have. As you can see, these are valuable things that we cannot forget.

Jesus announced that he had come to fulfill the law and not to abolish it, but he did not teach his disciples a series of steps to be better believers. He lived a lifestyle of faith with them. Jesus was with his disciples even in the most difficult moments, but he did not gather them together to give them a talk on obedience. He obeyed the Father in everything, and thus taught them to do the same.

*This is the covenant I will make with them after that
time, says the Lord. I will put my laws in their hearts,
and I will write them on their minds.*

(Hebrews 10:16)

PRIOR TRAINING FOR DISCIPLERS

Your church and ministry can do transformational discipleship and this preliminary training is intended to:

- Break any incorrect paradigm that exists around biblical discipleship in the understanding of your team members.

- Excite and encourage your volunteers with the challenging and wonderful project of making your participants more like Jesus.

- Optimize the growth process by establishing clear results for your ministry.

- Expand the vision of all those involved, recovering the sense of community of the first-century church.

ESSENTIAL PRINCIPLES OF BIBLICAL DISCIPLESHIP

WE ARE THE CHURCH

The greatest gift a church can receive is to have a group of families who take their responsibilities with such Christian seriousness that they are willing to completely alter their lifestyle to raise up disciples for Jesus Christ.

Abraham Kuyper

For a long time, we got so used to having meetings in a temple as part of the natural exercise of the church that this inertia produced in us a forgetfulness. We forgot we must be and make disciples, and not just attend meetings. In a biblical sense, the church is not a place to go, but a family to belong to, and if we fail to see it in this way, we will end up stunting our personal growth and that of the church.

The way we speak exhibits how we think and, consequently, how we act. Look at this conversation.

—What church do you go to?

—I attend Central Church.

—But... are you one of those who serve?

— I only attend, I am not in any ministry.

THE CHURCH IS NOT A PLACE TO GO, BUT A FAMILY TO BELONG TO.

Surely you heard something similar. But the truth is that "attending" an ecclesial community is practically impossible from God's perspective. Think of your family.

Do you attend your family weekly or are you part of it? Being part of the church and congregating is not the same as attending.

A biblical answer to the above question would be:

—I do not attend a church; I *am* the church of Christ.

Another very common comment is the following:

—I didn't go to church this week.

And their leader replies: —Well, you shouldn't miss it because remember we shouldn't stop congregating.

Nobody has bad intentions when saying these things but doing so can push the new generations to lead a double life. What exactly is congregate? Obviously, the word means to come together but in a biblical sense it means to be linked. Share a feeling, a belief, and a practical coexistence.

SAYING "WE ARE THE CHURCH" LETS US KNOW THAT WE ARE PART OF THE CHURCH AND WE WILL NEVER STOP BEING SO.

We must avoid having on one side of life: church meetings in which everyone is good, helpful, and even a good example for others, while having on the other side the "secular life." We have lived in that dichotomy for centuries, and it is time to say that it is wrong and that it is not biblical because, according to the written Word, there is no Christian life and secular life. If you are a disciple of Jesus then you are in whatever place, moment, condition, and activity; and everything you do you must do for the Lord (Colossians 3:23-24).

The phrase "go to church" makes us think that it is a destination to visit, a good place to hang out on certain days of the week. Instead, saying "we are the church" lets us know that we are a part of the church, and we never stop being so, no matter where we are or whom we are with.

Look at the following text from your Bible:

> The God who made the world and everything in it is the Lord of heaven and earth and does not live in temples built by human hands. And he is not served by human hands, as if he needed anything. Rather, he himself gives everyone life and breath and everything else. From one man he made all the nations, that they should inhabit the whole earth; and he marked out their appointed times in history and the boundaries of their lands. God did this so that they would seek him and perhaps reach out for him and find him, though he is not far from any one of us. "For in him we live and move and have our being". As some of your own poets have said, "We are his offspring."
> (Acts 17:24-28)

God is not always in the temples, but he is always in the church.

Many find it difficult to understand this phrase because they consider the temple as a synonym for church, but it is not. We are the church! What verse 28 says is compelling: "'For in him we live and move and have our being.' As some of your own poets have said, 'We are his offspring.'" God is in the church, so he dwells in us, and we are a part of his family.

GOD IS NOT ALWAYS IN THE TEMPLES, BUT HE IS ALWAYS IN THE CHURCH.

We gather in temples, yes, but God is not there because of the place; he is there because of us, his church. True disciples never cease to be the church and that is precisely why they are aware that they must be an active part of the meetings. They know how important community life is, they are a part of the body, they relate to others, and they serve God with their gifts and talents. But their mission does not end there. The disciple looks inside themself, examines themself periodically, and renders an account to their discipler based on the growth steps that the individual has taken. For this reason, although one participates in the meetings, **a disciple does not depend on the meeting to grow and fulfill what Christ has entrusted to them.**

Attending a congregation does not require you to be a disciple but BEING PART of a community of followers of Jesus requires you to be a disciple wherever you are, and requires you to fulfill the mission of making other disciples! No matter what community of believers you belong to, the mission remains the same, and you remain a part of the global church. We are all united in the same faith, purpose, and mission.

This perspective is born from understanding that the church is not a place limited to a physical space, but is a living organism and, as such, must grow integrally, as well as reproduce, multiply, and expand. If this does not happen, it is because we are doing something wrong.

Remember that just being a disciple of Jesus is not God's complete plan for you. It is also necessary to make disciples, model the character of Christ to others, accompany them to live this process, and encourage them to duplicate themselves in others.

PARADIGM SHIFTS

- I do not attend a church; I AM the church.

- The building where we meet is NOT the church, it is a temple.

- The church is not a static place; it is a LIVING organism.

- The church is made up of the children of God, wherever they come together. Whether that's in a large auditorium, in a park, or in a house, wherever the children of God are, that is where the church is.

IMPLEMENT IDEAS THAT CHANGE THE CULTURE

- Put up posters in the temple with phrases that help everyone change their mindset from "going to church" to "being the church."

- Try to repeat these phrases several times in meetings until the concepts become part of the habitual language.

- Work with all ministry members and volunteers so that in classes, small group meetings, and even individual counseling it is clearly stated that everything we Christians do every day has to do with the church.

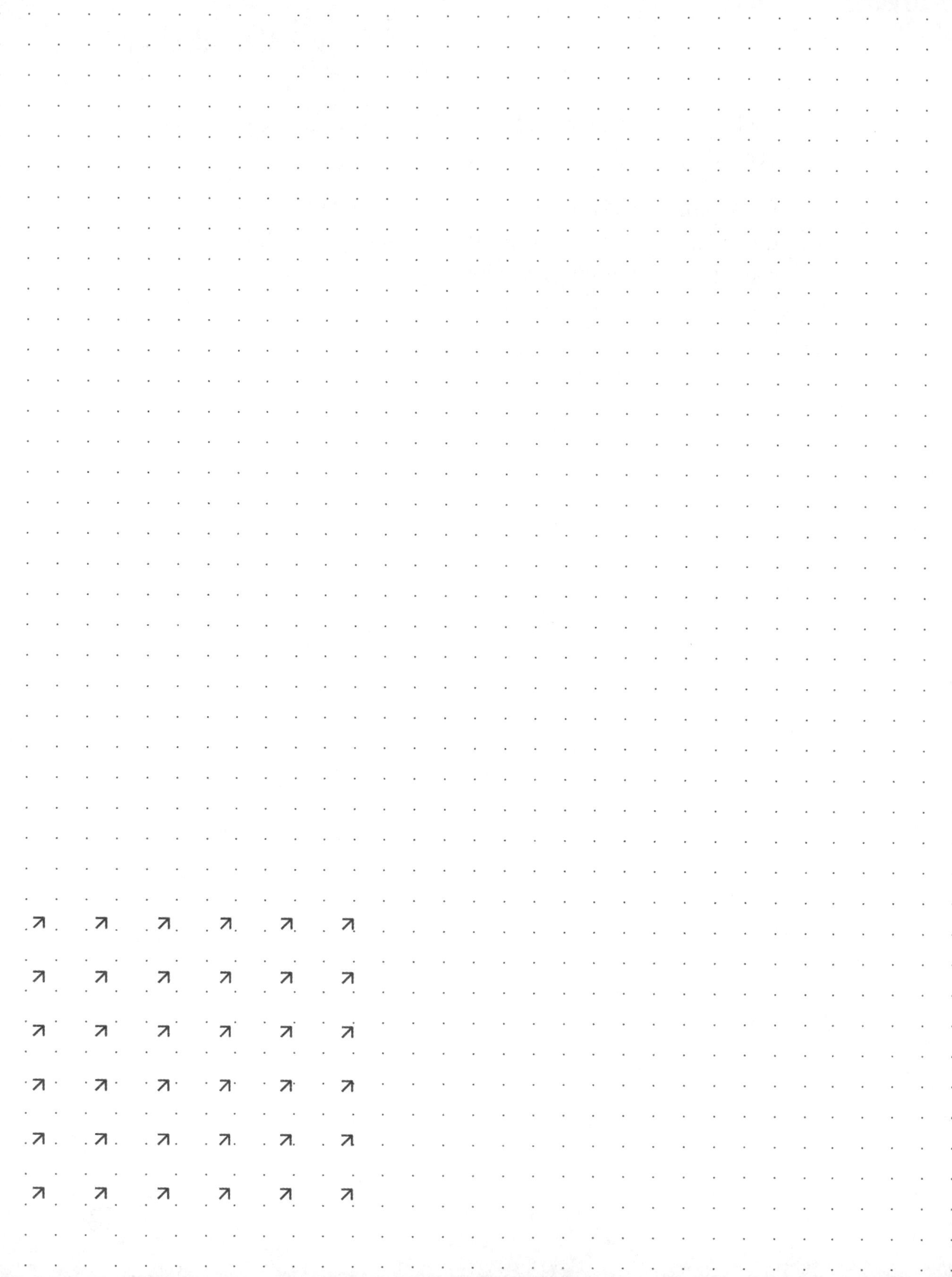

PRINCIPLE 2

TEACHING AND DISCIPLESHIP ARE NOT THE SAME THING

A Christian understanding of the world sees a child´s character not as genetically determined but as shaped to a significant degree by parental discipleship and discipline.

Russell D. Moore

It is easy to mix up teaching and discipleship because teaching is part of discipleship, but it is essential to differentiate between them. While discipleship uses teaching, teaching alone does not make disciples.

The practical reality of today's Christians is that we are bombarded by an enormous amount of diverse information, messages, and teachings on multiple networks. We have everything, and we idolize those who "speak better" and have popular social followings, but. . . how are we making disciples? Obviously, we don't want to judge anyone's character, but it's good to be clear that speaking well for a limited amount of time in a video or on a stage is not the same as doing what Jesus commanded us to do. Discipling is more than just speaking well.

Perhaps the key is not to stay in the discursive part of communication. Both authors of this book worked on this material because we want to help you include personal challenges in your teaching and in that intentional process which we are calling discipleship.

The personal or collective challenges that put into practice what has been learned in a relationship optimize results.

Reflect with your team on these differences between teaching and discipleship:

TEACHING	DISCIPLESHIP
Transmits knowledge.	Transmits a culture.
Is limited to classes and does not require much of a relationship with the teacher.	Aims for accompaniment and requires a relationship with the discipler.
Is based on knowing what the Bible or theology says.	Is based on practicing what the Bible says.
Leads you to greater knowledge.	Leads you to maturity in Christ.
Is a short moment or stage of life aimed to finish a program, training, or class.	Is a process that focuses on one's character.

If you pay attention to this chart, you can see that discipleship takes much more effort and time than teaching. Teachers are a key part of the process, but if you really want to disciple others, you are going to have to move to a new level of commitment and relationship. The process can start with teaching, but it doesn't end there.

WHOEVER EXERCISES THE INTENTIONAL PROCESS OF DISCIPLESHIP ASSUMES TRAITS OF SPIRITUAL PATERNITY.

Can you be a teacher and not be making disciples? Yes. When you limit teaching to the imparting of information, then the Word becomes a theory, and that conformism prevents God's truth from being real and alive in the person's life.

When you understand this and change the way you teach, then everything you teach will bear more fruit, since it will point toward the goal of making disciples and not just creating clones that know everything you already know. Additionally, at the end of the road, we are sure that you will be taught by each disciple too, because you never stop being one!

Someone who disciples is much more than a teacher. Little by little they become an example of life, a counselor, a coach, and a friend. Whoever exercises the intentional process of discipleship assumes traits of spiritual paternity since they assign identity, provide, and protect.

PARADIGM SHIFTS

- Teaching is not the "whole point" of discipleship.

- The driving force of discipleship is the relationships, not the knowledge.

- Knowing the Bible does not bring maturity; living it does.

IMPLEMENT IDEAS THAT CHANGE THE CULTURE

- Begin to differentiate biblical classes from discipleship processes.

- Instruct all involved (leaders, volunteers, and participants) to understand the difference.

- Identify those in your congregation who can be disciplers and train them with this guide.

- Make sure that all classes point to changes of action that will be monitored in a relationship.

EVERY DISCIPLE IS DIFFERENT

Fortunately, God made all varieties of people with a wide variety of interests and abilities. He has called people of every race and color who have been hurt by life in every manner imaginable. Even the scars of past abuse and injury can be the means of bringing healing to another. What wonderful opportunities to make disciples!

Charles R. Swindoll

The Greek philosophy that we inherited in the West from the Roman Empire gave us the not-so-astute idea that education should be like a funnel through which we all go in differently and then we all come out the same. Some have unknowingly sought this type of approach for discipleship and the church.

For this reason, programs are created with the expectation that every believer can complete them and become the same as all other Christians. However, today it is clear that we are all the same in essence, but we are all unique and we must all be brought to discipleship. Recognizing this is a good thing! Every disciple is different, has specific needs, and struggles with things that others don't. Their strengths and weaknesses are unique, and it is not possible to create a program that can serve everyone equally.

EVERY DISCIPLE IS DIFFERENT, HAS SPECIFIC NEEDS, AND STRUGGLES WITH THINGS THAT OTHERS DON'T.

In turn, the disciplers are aware of their own weaknesses in order to depend more on Christ, assume their strengths to be imparted to their followers, and are all fully guided by the Spirit of God.

It is for this reason that discipleship is more about personal development than just a collective group development. The group and the individual must be two complementary parts because it is not one or the other but both. There are truths that are better learned communally and others that must be taught face-to-face in the intimacy of two people. The challenge is that almost all church programs are made up of a big or small collective of people and there is little one-on-one approach. This is why it is so vital to remember that intimate conversations, personal encounters, and one-on-one challenges are a mark of genuine discipleship.

Some ideas to disciple on a personal level:

- Don't look at numbers, look at people.

- Create opportunities that go outside of a class setting.

- Create appropriate intentional intimacy as opposed to waiting for it to come naturally.

- Find out the interests of each disciple.

- If you want a genuine relationship, be authentic.

- Invest more into those who show greater interest and enthusiasm.

- Teach them to be accountable for their lives. This is imperative.

- Celebrate their successes; comfort them in their setbacks.

- Work on specific actions.

- Help them set/focus on personal goals.

- Assist them in depending on the Holy Spirit to be their guide.

These tips will vary slightly if you are discipling children, preteens, teens, or young adults. Each of the following principles will assist you in discovering the superior point of focus for each of the age groups. There is, however, no age limitation for someone to become a disciple.

PARADIGM SHIFTS

- To God we are all equal, but we are also different and unique.

- Discipleship always becomes a personal relationship.

- The weekly meetings do not disciple; the relationship does.

- We were created in the image and likeness of a multiform God.

IMPLEMENT IDEAS THAT CHANGE THE CULTURE

- Know the individual differences of the people who are in your discipleship group.

- Intentionally be aware of which paradigm is important to transfer value to them.

- Help the people you disciple get to know each other better.

- Create a conscious awareness of inclusion and integration in the members of your discipleship projects.

- Model a personalized pastoral approach.

DISCIPLESHIP IS FOR EVERY AGE

Jesus spent time and had close and personal relationships with his disciples. Do we have personal relationships with the new generations in our churches?

La Verne Tolbert

It seems that the general conscience of many congregations demands that we "seriously" disciple adults, while children, preteens, teens, and young adults can wait, and this is a strategic error with dire consequences. In fact, when it comes to transmitting culture, the best age is the youngest. When you work with adults you will find that it is a little more difficult to change something that they have done in a certain and determined way for their entire lives. Instead, the youngest are moldable, teachable, and adaptable. They know that they don't know, and that's good.

If you have an influential position with the new generations, God has held you in high esteem.

Now, working with children is not the same as working with young adults, so here are some recommendations that correspond to the 4 basic work areas of an intelligent vision for generational pastoral care.

WHEN IT COMES TO TRANSMITTING CULTURE, THE BEST AGE IS THE YOUNGEST.

FOR THE DISCIPLESHIP OF CHILDREN

- Work closely with parents. They are the natural leaders and disciplers that God gave children. Discipling children is cooperating with their parents.

- Help children share their growth steps in the context of their family.

- Use multiple sources, so the training process will be comprehensive and will reach everyone. (If you want to know more about multiple intelligences, take advantage of the course at the e625 online Institute.)

FOR THE DISCIPLESHIP OF PRETEENS

- This is the stage where we begin to see the world beyond just the home and with the arrival of abstract thought we begin to question the validity of what we learned in childhood. For this reason, teaching must move from concrete data to abstract principles.

- At this stage it is also crucial to collaborate with their parents because this is the last great opportunity they will have to shape desired values and habits in their children. In the following stages of their lives, instilling values becomes more difficult.

- The relationship with their leaders and teachers must now be more personal. They need models and it is very possible that the models they have at this stage will continue to subconsciously be their example for the rest of their lives.

FOR THE DISCIPLESHIP OF TEENS

- The relationship of boys and girls with their parents is always important, but the relationship with their friends at this age is key. Communal discipleship is most significant at this stage.

- Naturally, in adolescence we all question our family framework and leaders should not throw more fuel on the fire but rather help them positively make that evaluation.

- Be prepared to talk with them about feelings and emotions. Their life during this stage is going to be a roller coaster of emotional ups and downs and they will need someone mature, and therefore stable, to accompany them.

FOR THE DISCIPLESHIP OF YOUNG ADULTS

- To the same degree that communal discipleship is vital in the previous stage, mentorship is vital in this young adult phase. A mentor meets their deepest needs and allows space to ask difficult questions, even the most intimate questions.

- Present options to young adults without giving them orders and, above all, without making decisions for them. Teach them to make their decisions based on the Word of God. Coaching is a good discipline to add to your skills and in the e625.com online institute you can find foundational generational coaching courses.

- In this stage, most consider pursuing a profession, choosing a marriage partner, planning for the future, and discovering one's life purpose (or even a ministerial calling). These are the talking points in the discipleship relationship with young adults.

PARADIGM SHIFTS

- Age is not a limitation to making disciples, but it is necessary to adapt according to the stage.

- Discipling adults is not more valuable than discipling little ones.

- The transferring of culture takes time, focus, and effort.

IMPLEMENT IDEAS THAT CHANGE THE CULTURE

- Work on a vision of *Generational Leadership.*[1] (If you haven't read this book we recommend you do so as soon as possible.) Join the adult ministries with those in your congregation who are dedicated to the new generations and plan an activity that focuses on making the discipleship of new generations a priority for your entire church, as it was commissioned by God in Deuteronomy 6. Coordinating efforts from time to time does wonders for the heart and minds of co-laborers.

- Organize things in a way that each of the new generational stages leads a meeting one or more times per year. Give preteens responsibilities, encourage teens to be an example for the little ones, train young adults to model behavior in teens, and provide examples of maturity to take firm steps toward the next stage in which they find themselves.

---

1. Lucas Leys, *Liderazgo Generacional.* (Dallas, Texas: Editorial e625, 2017).

DISCIPLESHIP HAPPENS IN PROCESSES

When the church becomes an end in itself, it ends. When any ministry, no matter how great, becomes an end goal, it ends. What we need is for discipleship to become the goal, and then the process of conversion and sanctification will never end.
Robby Gallaty

When we talk about discipling others, we must consider how to elevate our disciples' level of maturity. It is about going from one point to the next. This makes it necessary to draw a route that marks the steps of that sustained growth that we seek, while understanding that there are smaller steps along the way. When we understand this better, we focus less on our own assessment of events and pay more attention to a progressive view of processes.

It is one thing to learn a principle and quite another to live it. The first is an intellectual act, something that can be received in a class. To put a principle into practice, however, requires decision, effort, and the fulfillment of goals that help make the principle a part of our culture and way of life.

For this reason, someone who decides to disciple cannot be satisfied with teaching principles, since that is only the first part. It is necessary that these principles

WE FOCUS LESS ON OUR OWN ASSESSMENT OF EVENTS AND PAY MORE ATTENTION TO A PROGRESSIVE VIEW OF PROCESSES.

are part of the discipler's culture so that they can transmit them in such a way that they become part of the culture of the disciple.

It is a lifestyle that should arise naturally and not be forced.

THE PENTAGON OF LEARNING APPLIED TO DISCIPLESHIP

The book *Generational Leadership* describes the need to improve teaching methods from a relational nuance with the following pentagon:

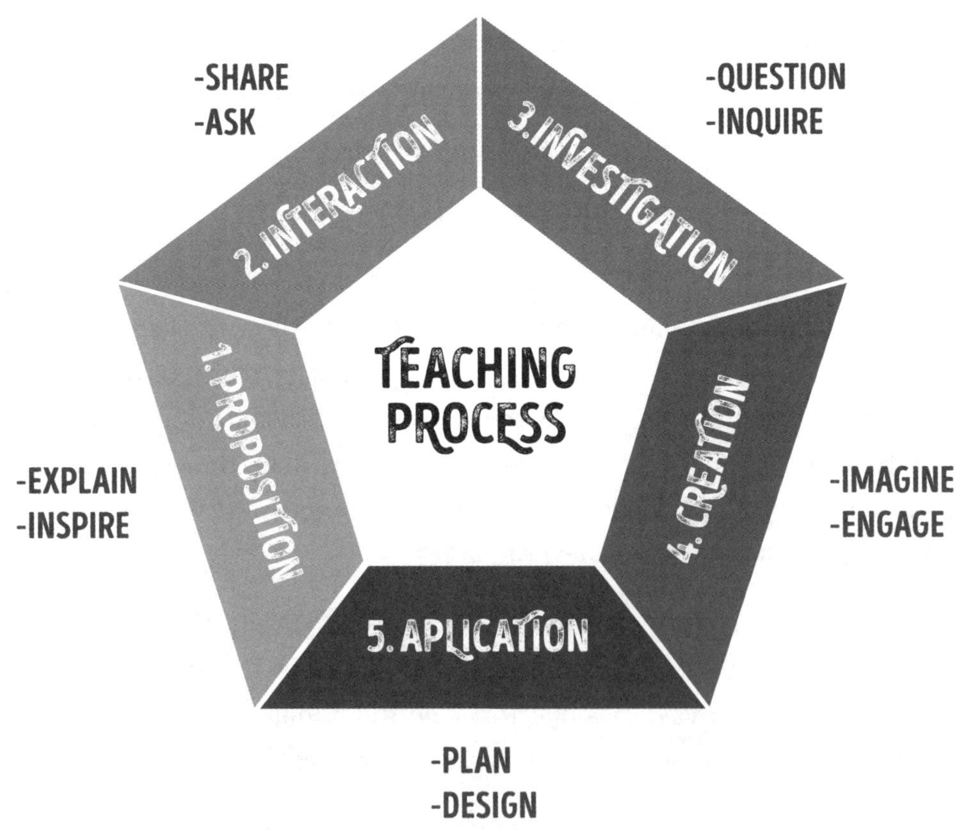

Each one of the sides of the pentagon marks a dimension of the action that the disciplers must observe. If you think about it well, you will understand the need to make disciples through processes, instead of just having students in a class.

Here's an example of how this process works:

1. **PROPOSITION:** Pick an aspect of the character of Christ.

2. **INTERACTION:** Explore the different appreciations of the aspect.

3. **INVESTIGATION:** Look up what the Bible says about it.

4. **CREATION:** Engage others in doing it together.

5. **APLICATION:** Live it in your own flesh and be accountable for it.

A process can be focused on a specific area of the disciple's life, on a specific theme, on an aspect of character, etc., In this way you can create different proposals for stages that adapt to the principles of this pentagon. Nothing is rigid. On the contrary, everything is adaptable and 100 percent improvable and you can read more in the book *Generational Leadership*.

Although this book may appear to speak to the project of making disciples, it is meant as a tool to help guide a long-term process whose final goal is to form the character of Christ in the life of the believer, which is entirely dependent on the relationship between discipler and disciple and their mutual commitment to the process.

PARADIGM SHIFTS

- Discipleship is not a propositional discourse but a process of internalizing truths that respect the different abilities of our brains to learn.

- The preacher shares a monologue, the teacher teaches a class, the discipler accompanies through stages.

- The relationship between disciplers and disciples is the very nature of discipleship.

IMPLEMENT IDEAS THAT CHANGE THE CULTURE

- Get used to creating processes. Preaching or lectures are not as effective in generating understanding for most people. Use series, long-term lessons, and various instances so that different people internalize the contents of what you want them to practice.

- The call is not to have meetings where we stand to sing and then listen to a lecture. Think outside the sanctuary, the classroom, and the speeches given.

PRINCIPLE 6

ACCOMPANIMENT AND MENTORSHIP

I believe in the transforming power of the Spirit of God and that Jesus can be formed in the life of the new generations. I work from his reality, not from fiction.

Félix Ortiz

According to what we can notice in the New Testament, the apostle Paul would come to a city, preach, and then continue working with a few select believers until he formed in them the character of Christ so that they would then do the same with others. When it was time, he left there but he did not disconnect from them: he continued to give them instructions through his writings.

If we are talking about relationships and processes, we must consider the development of relationships in phases or stages and that is why it is good to include the word project. If we want to form disciples with maturity, who truly reflect the character of Christ, we must first form the attributes of Christ in ourselves and then gradually develop each aspect of our personal commitments, modeling them in the lives of others. Paul said: "Be imitators of me, just as I am of Christ" and this can take years. At the same time, it is advisable to plan it with phases and times, and then release the disciples so that they go and repeat the process with others.

THE GREATEST WEALTH OF DISCIPLESHIP IS IN THE RELATIONSHIP.

The relationship with your disciples can last a lifetime, and they may even perceive you as a spiritual reference, but that does not necessarily mean that the roles are forever and that they will not grow past it. The point is to accompany them in this stage to help them take steps toward maturity they need to take in this period in which they find themselves. This "staying in touch" can use digital tools such as video chats, social media, and similar tools. But the point is to mentor, that is, model to transfer certain vital lessons that must be learned at a stage in life.

Look what the book of Exodus says about God's relationship with Moses. Although Moses could not look directly into the face of God because he would have died, his personal encounter with the Eternal God produced in him a weight of glory that others could not fail to recognize.

> *The Lord would speak to Moses face to face, as one speaks to a friend. Then Moses would return to the camp, but his young aide Joshua son of Nun did not leave the tent.*
> (Exodus 33:11)

In other words, being close to a good role model has an impact that sooner or later everyone will notice. Moses was discipled by God, just as all of us can be. This process is based on the relationship we reach with him. In the same way, we can all accompany others in their growth process.

PARADIGM SHIFTS

- There is no discipleship without accompaniment.

- The greatest wealth of discipleship is in the relationship.

- The discipleship relationship can last a lifetime, although roles usually change according to the stages of life.

IMPLEMENT IDEAS THAT CHANGE THE CULTURE

- Take personal time with each person you have in a discipleship group.

- Let the people in your group know aspects of your life that are outside of a weekly class.

- They should keep in mind from early on that one day they will have to disciple others. Thus, the change will not be left alone in your hands, since the responsibility of making disciples belongs to all believers.

- Create dscipleship projects for specific stages of life with measurable results.

PARENTS' INVOLVEMENT

We discipline our children not so that they will make us happy, but so that they will serve Christ as adults. We educate them not so they can have a good job, but to develop them to be the best follower of Jesus that they can be.
Chap Bettis

All Christian parents are involved in the discipleship of their children even if they don't know it or are unintentional about it. The job of every church leader is to make sure parents know this and help them to be intentional about doing it better.

As children grow, their ability and need to relate to other role models also grows. That is where we come in, not as something parallel to the family but rather by joining forces in a collaborative way. The point is that a constant interaction between leadership and parents goes much further than we might suspect. The role of the parents decreases as the children grow older and it is necessary for this to happen, because otherwise, they could never become mature children who effectively serve the kingdom of heaven. But again. . . this is a PROCESS. It could be slow moving, and we must be patient, but that is why, when we work

ALL CHRISTIAN PARENTS ARE INVOLVED IN THE DISCIPLESHIP OF THEIR CHILDREN EVEN IF THEY DON'T KNOW IT

on discipleship from the perspective of the church, we need to nurture a positive relationship with parents as well.

The role of each one could vary over time, in this way:

6–9	10–13	14–17	18–25

6–9
- Children are discipled by their parents.
- Parents are the clearest role model.
- Leaders support parents' leadership.
- Their contact with preteens is vital.

10–13
- Parents are important role models, as are leaders and teachers.
- Parents should get other adults to support their work.
- Their contact with positive teens is vital.

14–17
- Parents model.
- Leaders are mentors.
- Parents should relate with their children's friends.
- Contact with young adults who are good role models is vital.

18–25
- Parents and leaders delegate autonomy.
- Leaders must be life mentors and coaches for specific decisions.
- Contact with young married couples with good relationships is vital.

PARADIGM SHIFTS

- The role of parents changes as the ages advance.

- Leaders without the parents can't get very far.

- The parents must learn to lean on leaders.

IMPLEMENT IDEAS THAT CHANGE THE CULTURE

- Set a good pace for parent meetings based on the age of your students.

- Promote parent-child meetings more often. The interaction that this produces rescues God's design for the church.

- As a disciple, you must always think of each disciple within a family context. There will always be people close to you who can be a good influence on the development of the one you are discipling.

- Let non-Christian parents know that the church is there to help them in their parenthood.

THE MIRROR PRINCIPLE

Discipleship is the process of becoming who Jesus would be if He were you.
Dallas Willard

The apostle John made this principle clear: "Whoever claims to live in him must live as Jesus did" (1 John 2:6).

The first great commitment of those of us who dedicate ourselves to the discipleship project is to reflect Christ in everything: his character, passion, decisions, will, and transparency. That is why it is said that no one can disciple if they are not a disciple first. Anyone who is willing to be a disciple tries to look more like Jesus every day since he came, in turn, to reflect the Father. As Paul says, Christ is the image of the invisible God (Colossians 1:15).

The second great commitment is to extend this for others to also resemble Jesus. For this reason we have an exciting and enormous responsibility that can sometimes intimidate us, for which we must also learn from Jesus's dependence on God. In John 15:15 we find him saying: "I no longer call you servants, because a servant does not know his master's business. Instead, I have called you friends, for everything that I learned from my Father I have made known to you."

How good to know that we have a great and powerful God and that he continually renews his mercy for us because we will need it in this process. If we depend on him in the discipleship project, we will surely succeed!

If you think about it, you will see that creation has that same design. Everything that God created has his stamp of ownership. Everything resembles him. Everything was made by him, through him, and for him. Genesis tells the story of the creation of the human being, saying that they were made "in the image and likeness of God" That is, they were created as a mirror that reflects him and starting from this principle, we could design a discipleship process as follows:

1. I know one aspect of the character of Christ. For example: love.

2. I long to be like him in that way.

3. I stop loving my way, to start loving as he loved.

4. I battle against the arguments that prevent me from loving as he loved.

5. I live and practice his love.

6. I teach others to love like him.

7. I choose another aspect of Christ's character to imitate. And so the whole process begins again.

In this way, the discipleship process will last a lifetime, because in each aspect we can find a new depth in the next stage. It is good to be able to work on it with those we have been put in charge of.

PARADIGM SHIFTS

- Reflecting Jesus in our own lives is more important than giving a good sermon or class about Jesus. That means dying to myself so that he can live in me.

- All creation was made in the image of God, and we must and can recover that design.

- Reflecting Christ is not a feeling or a romantic lyric to a cute song but a concrete action in which you model his character.

IMPLEMENT IDEAS THAT CHANGE THE CULTURE

- Choose specific aspects of Jesus's character to reflect on, understand, and develop.

- Prepare a progressive and ordered teaching plan. Put up signs that say something like: "This is the month of love." You can use videos and images for this purpose, and testimonies can be given about experiences of giving and receiving love, so that everyone involved in the discipleship project is clear about the tangible objective that is being worked on.

> REFLECTING CHRIST IS NOT A FEELING OR A ROMANTIC LYRIC TO A CUTE SONG BUT A CONCRETE ACTION IN WHICH YOU MODEL HIS CHARACTER.

ACTIVITIES WITH A PURPOSE

*Renewing ourselves is not a luxury, it is a necessity for
every follower of Jesus in order to continue being agents
of restoration and reconciliation in a broken world.*

Félix Ortiz

When we mentally leave behind the sanctuary, the classroom, and the liturgy, our panorama expands to the point that we find new scenarios and possibilities to achieve the great purpose of discipleship, which is that the people we influence become more like Jesus.

For the best disciplers, everything is done with a purpose, both relationships and spontaneous conversations at every available opportunity, as well as good programs that facilitate the internalization of desired behaviors.

Some of these activities will be personal or relationship building for a small group. Others, however, should include the community. This is how we teach kids, pre-teens, teens, and young adults to be one body. There character problems will also be revealed, and they will learn to support each other. Then, the disciples will be aware of the reactions of the disciplers to continue forming Christ in them, and the disciplers will also keep an eye as the disciples to imitate them. In those situations, you will realize that they look at you more than you realize.

Remember that it is not about creative ideas just to be creative, or spectacular activities with the desire to be spectacular. From the point of view of the disciple, even the spectacle of a program is simply a pedagogical tool (and not for

LET US ASK GOD FOR WISDOM TO ENSURE THAT EACH ACTIVITY ALIGNS WITH HIS INTENTIONS FOR OUR MINISTRIES.

you to show off). The basic objectives are to promote coexistence, create interest, and facilitate practical lessons in which to model principles.

Think of all these activities from the perspectives of the purpose of discipleship and you will find a new dimension to them:

- Going for a walk outside

- Playing sports

- Climbing a mountain

- Going swimming

- Planting or caring for a tree or plant

- Reading a book

- Visiting the sick, elderly, or orphans

- Watching a movie

- Going to the theater, circus, dance, etc.

- Carrying out a carpentry project

- Playing or singing a song that you can discuss together

- Visiting a relative

The possibilities are endless.

Let us ask God for wisdom to ensure that each activity aligns with his intentions for our ministries.

PARADIGM SHIFTS

- Exercise, play, and fellowship are excellent ministry tools when done with a purpose.

- The activities planned outside the sanctuary are as rich and necessary as those that take place inside.

- Discipleship is not reduced to listening, but disciples must see and act. That is why it is necessary to create these moments with our programs.

IMPLEMENT IDEAS THAT CHANGE THE CULTURE

- Plan for the long term and share the plan with everyone you can.

- Present a public report of all the activities you facilitate outside the sanctuary. It is always better when everyone finds out about the riches that are achieved in personal discipleship.

- Insistently convey to everyone involved in your ministry the idea that your mission is not for them to listen to a biblical proposition quietly and just say amen. It promotes a culture of coexistence, actions, and experiences and not only of sermons and classes.

THE CALL IS FOR EVERYONE

Discipleship is not a choice.

Tim Keller

To think that only pastors have the call to disciple others is nonsense. The great commission to go and make disciples (Matthew 28:16-20; Mark 16:14-18; Luke 24:36-49; John 20:19-23) was given to all the disciples.

If we acknowledge Jesus as our Lord and Savior, then we have a call to discipleship.

All Christians must disciple and doing so is one of the most tremendous ways we can grow because we all learn by teaching. We have all received something that we can give and have learned something that we can teach. Along the way, some are filled with fear or justifications, thinking that they must prepare a lot or that they could make a mistake. But the reality is that we are all in the process of learning because we never stop being disciples, and of course we are going to make mistakes. That is neither something new, nor is it a tragedy.

If Christ trusts us for this task, it must be because we can do it.

If the church continues to believe that one sermon is enough to make disciples, then we will continue to see burnt-out pastors and continue to turn good preachers into celebrities because they speak well, even if they don't help us achieve what God wants us to achieve. God wants disciples and not people with good

IF WE ACKNOWLEDGE JESUS AS OUR LORD AND SAVIOR, THEN WE HAVE A CALL TO DISCIPLESHIP.

morals and some biblical knowledge to behave like Christians in the temple on the weekend.

Disciples.

The sermons, the songs, and the temple are tools and not objectives and when they are used well, they help us to produce disciples of Jesus. And the great news is that there are other tools and mechanisms modeled by Jesus himself to achieve it.

This is where the most important action of all appears: being a model. Modeling is something that adults and even young adults always do for the new generations even if we are not aware that we are doing it. The entire proposal of Generational Leadership is linked to this reality and invites us to be intentional with it. All Christian adults are involved in the discipleship of the youth although perhaps without knowing it. The young adults are ready to disciple the teens because they are already modeling for them what the next stage is all about and the teens, in turn, are doing the same with the preteens and the preteens are being watched by the kids. Modeling is a natural process, and it is much more effective when we are aware of it and do it with devotion, wit, and fidelity.

PARADIGM SHIFTS

- Discipleship is the task of all God's children.

- Pastors and leaders who do not move everyone to disciple sooner or later will burn out or become superficial, or both.

- Discipleship is something that we may already be doing without realizing it, but that we can improve exponentially if we start doing it intentionally.

IMPLEMENT IDEAS THAT CHANGE THE CULTURE

- The importance of discipleship must be communicated privately, publicly, and continually.

- Delegate authority and don't just focus on your work team and volunteers.

- Celebrate what God celebrates and not what the world already celebrates (such as fame, recognition, beauty, or eloquence).

- Involve new generations in ministry and discipleship at an early age. They are already looking at us.

10 LESSONS FOR DISCIPLING PRETEENS

Discipleship is a call to an exciting adventure, and it is also a huge challenge.

The preteens stage is characterized by the enormous amount of emotions, ideas, thoughts, and choices that arise in the development of identity. When we work in the discipleship of teenagers, we are building the foundations of character and personality that will govern their lives in the future. For this reason, each lesson that we carry out, each meeting, and each individual space for mentoring and accompaniment, must be an intentional moment to affirm their identity in Christ and their character on that rock. In addition, we must manage to give the disciples all the necessary tools so that they never get stuck in religious inertia.

The following lessons are designed under the sequence or model "AFFIRM" which uses the process developed in the following acrostic:

 **A**valanche of ideas

 **F**oundations of the theme

 **F**ocus on truth

 **I**ntrospection

 **R**eflect on a character

 **M**obilize

This "AFFIRM" model facilitates a discipleship process in which both teachers and each learner are challenged to grow and mature.

These are details for each stage:

1. **Avalanche of ideas.** It collects diverse opinions about the proposed topic: what is heard among teens, what is said in the streets, and what society perceives from different points of view.

2. **Foundations of the theme.** It is a compendium of theoretical foundations that help us clarify ideas and generate biblical, scientific, and philosophical support on the proposed topic.

3. **Focus on truth.** Contains the necessary biblical development to form the teenager in the principles of the Word of God. The expressed criteria point to teenagers being able to find the answers to the problems of life in Scripture.

4. **Introspection.** This includes questions that help the teen to acquire an adequate criterion on the subject based on their own analysis. You can include open discussions to hear the opinions of other members of the group.

5. **Reflect on a character.** In this section we are committed to talking about two characters. The first will be a current character, known and admired among teens, and the second will be a biblical character.

6. **Mobilize.** Here discipler and disciple generate together a list of specific actions to be implemented after finishing the lesson. In this way, the topic does not remain theoretical, but encourages the preteens to put what they have learned into practice.

This sequence will also help you create other topics and lessons or enhance other materials that you can access on www.e625.com.

The one who leads the discipleship (you!) must study the lesson and delve into it to later determine the treatment to give at each step. Some topics will be hotter and more urgent, depending on the disciples' context, so some lessons could last one, two, or three weeks, depending on what you, your team, and the Holy Spirit dictate.

That's right.

It will be essential for each discipler to walk in a close relationship with the Holy Spirit so that they can be guided by him and thus impact a new generation of disciples.

WARNING:

From here we assume that you have already carefully read the essential principles of biblical discipleship in Session 1, and that all members of your team have gone through prior tactical training to carry out the lessons that begin below.

We already made it clear that parents are the first to be called to disciple their children, so it's not a bad idea for you to start this material with a mini training for them as well, or at least with a presentation informing them that you will be sharing the following lessons from this discipleship project with your children.

This project tries to mobilize more people to take up the challenge of not continuing to sit in a religious comfort, but to help the generations that come next, inside and outside the meetings or sanctuaries.

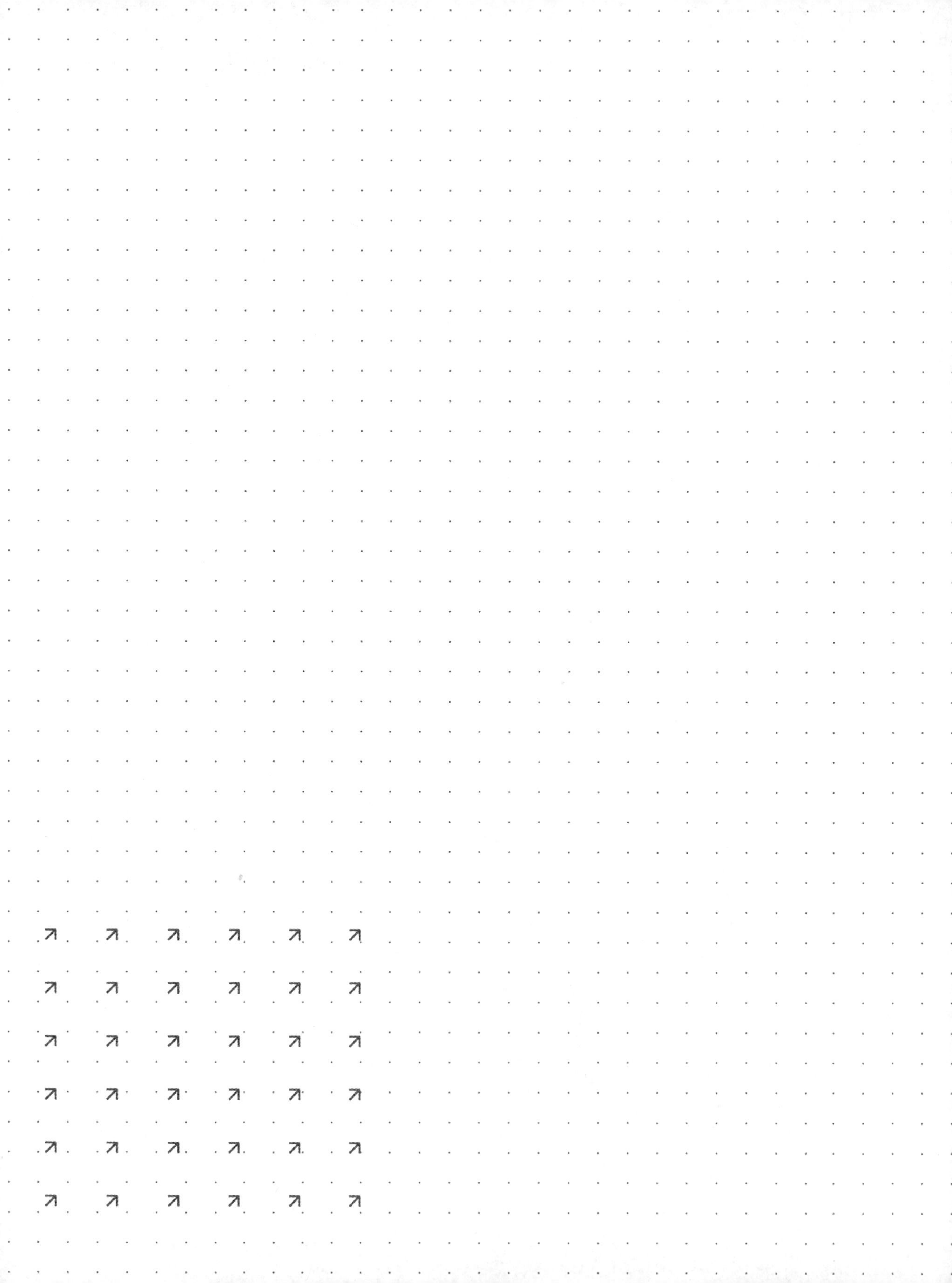

LESSON 1

AN EMOTIONAL ADVENTURE

*Everything you think and do is tinged with
the color of emotions.*

Karen Lacota, *Women's decisions*

God is interested in us not only admitting his existence, but living like Jesus, and the preteen stage is something of an intellectual adventure, since now the boys and girls want to find out the reason for the stories, and not just who the characters of the Bible were and what they each did.

Now they need to connect the Bible with their personal history, the one that they are starting to learn about more precisely. This, in turn, is going to start giving them some anxiety and vertigo, and that is why it is vital that they learn to work with their emotions as soon as possible.

AVALANCHE OF IDEAS

Introductory activities are ideal for connecting the group with the topic to be discussed. This time we will start with the following.

Prepare pictures showing different types of emotional reactions (laughter, crying, disgust, anger, discouragement, etc.). Divide the group in two and organize a competition. The group that can best recreate the emotion of each picture will win a point. When they are ready, start showing the pictures.

Remind them that their reactions will have to be very exaggerated if they want to win. Encourage them to try their best during the activity but be sure to finish the activity before they get bored.

If your meeting is virtual, you don't need to split the group in two, and the activity can be done in a way that produces the same effect. In this case, we suggest you pass the photos, one by one, in a group chat that you have previously created, and then in the meeting everyone can play showing the different reactions with their faces. Since everyone is looking at each other, the result will be the same.

After that, pose these hypothetical situations and ask them to tell you what they would feel in each of them:

- Driving a racecar.

- Winning an Oscar or Grammy.

- Catching the eye of the models walking down a catwalk.

- Going skydiving.

- When your team wins the international championship.

- When the person you like makes eye contact with you.

- When something embarrassing happens to you.

- The divorce of your parents.

- When someone betrays your trust.

- The death of a person you cared about.

The question is always, "How would this make you feel?" Depending on your group, you can even challenge them to act out these situations in pairs (and you'll be surprised how many good actors and actresses you have).

Note that the examples, although they do not follow a strict order, go from joy to sadness. Take time to explore each idea until the group can feel some emotion. Try to get them to imagine the situation by closing their eyes, or, as we said earlier, acting out the situations.

At the end, and if it did not already arise naturally, you can ask two of them to talk about a personal memory in which they experienced a very strong emotion.

FOUNDATIONS OF THE THEME

Emotions can be like a roller coaster, full of highs and lows, violent ups, and spaces of relative calm. For this reason, imagine the different reactions that people feel when they are on a roller coaster and mix them all together. That's what it's like to be in the mind of a preteen.

Their stories seen through the eyes of their parents is different, but the parents don't suffer less than their kids. They are often disconcerted to see that their sons and daughters have ceased to be boys and girls and have become some kind of scary monster they don't want to face. The reactions of this monster, moreover, are intense, sudden, and for no apparent reason. Unfortunately, most parents view these emotional outbursts as disrespectful or as signs of rebellion. And it is logical that they think that, because many of their children's reactions can become offensive.

IN THE MIND OF A PRETEEN, THERE IS A MIX OF EMOTIONS SIMILAR TO THOSE THAT PEOPLE EXPERIENCE ON ROLLER COASTERS.

The secret to help parents cope with this dramatic stage in the best possible way is for them to know that much of what their children say and do is not planned, nor is it a stage they will be in forever.

Little by little, these mood swings will be controlled by a more mature spirit, which will develop in them as the discipleship yields results (although, to be clear, it should not be your intention for them to stop being preteens, because per God's design, that's the stage they're at!).

You can help your group move along this path of maturity by teaching them a little about feelings and emotions. A good explanation of the difference between these two words is as follows:

Emotions are intense and short-lived. They carry a large dose of hormones and, just as they appear suddenly, in the same way they disappear. Some examples of emotions can be anger, joy, rage, or passion.

Feelings are slower to appear, they arise little by little, and the experience is maintained for a longer time. For example: the illusion of falling in love, sadness, mild anger, or frustration. In any case, some feelings can become very intense and stay that way for a long time, and some can even turn into pathologies such as depression.

This is what you should make very clear to preteens regarding their emotions at this stage:

- It is a stage of emotional ups and downs. It is normal that one day you are fine and the next day you feel worse.

- These mood swings have no apparent reason, they just happen.

- The world is not your enemy. Even if you feel that nobody understands you, humanity is not against you.

- Nobody is looking at you weirdly. Don't think that because you're going through your preteens, you're some rare specimen that everyone wants to stare at. We've all been there.

- There are always people around you who can be of help if you need to vent. You just have to choose them well.

Something to remember is that we must also be connected with their parents. Many times, preteens experience situations in which they need the ones they love the most to be willing to listen and love them unconditionally. Parents must be trained in this, and warned about the emotional changes that their children are experiencing or will experience.

📖 FOCUS ON TRUTH

There are some emotions that are positive, while others can be dangerous if we let them fester. The Word of God, contains some advice on this, as it does for all aspects of life, advice that can help us to better understand and manage our emotions. Let's look at, for example, Proverbs 15. (You can read the whole chapter if you want to go deeper with your group, but we'll just look at a few verses here.)

"A gentle answer turns away wrath, but a harsh word stirs up anger." (v.1)
"A happy heart makes the face cheerful, but heartache crushes the spirit." (v.13)
"All the days of the oppressed are wretched, but the cheerful heart has a continual feast." (v.15)
"A hot-tempered person stirs up conflict, but the one who is patient calms a quarrel." (v.18)

As you can see, the book of Proverbs contains a lot of wisdom! Here we chose these four verses to show examples of emotions and how to handle them:

- Verse 1 tells us about anger. We can all get angry, but there is a real and 100% effective alternative to calm another person's anger, and that is to respond kindly.

- Verse 13 tells us about joy and a happy heart. Joy can change a person's face. But there is also the antithesis, sadness, which can provoke a person's spirit to become troubled.

- Verse 15 speaks of afflictions and sadness. There is not a single person in the world who does not feel sadness, and it is good to feel it when there are legitimate causes such as the death of a loved one. But we must learn to channel it positively, and never lose the joy that gratitude produces.

- Verse 18 talks about anger again and how it relates to fighting. But it also presents us with a hopeful fact: anger can be controlled!

Now let's look at a text in which Paul speaks to the believers in the Corinthian church about sadness:

> Godly sorrow brings repentance that leads to salvation and leaves no regret, but worldly sorrow brings death.
>
> **2 Corinthians 7:10**

Here the apostle Paul is making a play on words and establishing a contrast. There are two types of sadness. The one that has to do with guilt, which is dissipated with repentance, and the other, the sadness of the world, which has to do with the anxiety that society transmits and that does not produce anything good in us.

When we sin, the Holy Spirit speaks to our conscience, and fills us with sadness with the aim of leaving the sin and getting closer to God (which, for Paul and for the Bible in general, is synonymous with life). On the contrary, the sadness that the world produces is usually a by-product of anxiety for not feeling loved enough, and that comes by, and kills our hearts.

So let's also talk about love!!

The Word of God says many things about love, but something that is extremely important is knowing how to distinguish between spiritual love and sentimental or romantic love. They are two different things.

LOVE, AS A HUMAN EMOTION, HAS ITS LIMITATIONS, BUT THE LOVE WE LEARN FROM GOD IS WILD!

Romantic love is a human feeling that brings you closer to a person with the intention of establishing a relationship, although we also emotionally love close people with whom we have experienced important things. In the preteen stage, with the accumulation of emotions and feelings that are mixed, triggering unpredictable attitudes and behaviors, it is necessary for boys and girls to realize that it is not a stage in which love of this nature can be handled wisely. Many preteens make the mistake of thinking that they can handle it.

But let's also talk about spiritual love, or agape love. This is a different love, which is not limited to human emotions, but transcends to eternity. This kind of love helps us make mature and conscious decisions.

> "My command is this: Love each other as I have loved you. Greater love has no one than this: to lay down one's life for one's friends. You are my friends if you do what I command."
> **John 15:12-14**

What a powerful verse! It tells us that love, as a human emotion, has its limitations, but the love we learn from God is wild! No kind of human love is greater than that of someone who gives their life for someone else. On the other hand, verse 14 tells us that we will be considered friends of God (in agape love) if we do what he commands us, that is, if we are obedient.

It's interesting to note that for human beings love is usually measured based on what we feel, while genuine and spiritual love is measured based on how obedient we are to God's instructions. We can also see that when there is no agape love in people's lives, they get carried away by erotic, passionate, sentimental, human, and limited love.

Which kind of love would you like to be loved with?

Which kind of love do you have for others?

Emotions compete within us to get out, and we can choose to feed the best of them.

 INTROSPECTION

The following activity will be helpful in getting your preteens thinking. Place some words that represent as many emotions as possible somewhere that everyone can see them. You can prepare posters or write them on a whiteboard. You can also use the images from the initial activity.

Now, let's play mimicking emotions!

Have them each take a poster, or choose one of the words on the board, and on the count of three they all do an exaggerated mime of that emotion. If your meeting is virtual, place all the words in a chat and ask them to choose one of them from that list. But they must all do it together, at the same time! Then switch emotions, and repeat the activity several times, until everyone has gone through each of the words.

Then continue with the second part of the activity. Ask your preteens to think about which of these emotions tends to be the most intense for each of them, and why that happens. Now, each one should take the poster that represents that emotion and share a few reasons why they identify with it. You can also encourage them to share a personal story in which they experienced their chosen emotion. Give them a couple of minutes to think.

It usually takes time for preteens to dive into sharing things that are personal but give them a chance.

Controlling emotions in the preteen stage may seem like a massive challenge, but it's not impossible. One of the keys to achieve this is knowing the goodness of the Spirit of God in us. When you observe the list of manifestations of the fruit of the Spirit in the book of Galatians, you will see that they have a lot to do with a development in the spiritual dimension of each person, which helps them to manage emotions properly.

CONTROLLING EMOTIONS IN THE PRETEEN STAGE MAY SEEM LIKE A MASSIVE CHALLENGE, BUT IT'S NOT IMPOSSIBLE.

> "But the fruit of the Spirit is love, joy, peace, forbearance, kindness, goodness, faithfulness, *gentleness and self-control. Against such things there is no law.*"
>
> **Galatians 5:22–23**

Try the exercise of writing a list of the manifestations of the fruit of the Spirit of God and, at the same time, identify the possible emotions that are related to them.

MANIFESTATIONS OF THE FRUIT OF THE SPIRIT OF GOD	RELATED HUMAN EMOTIONS AND FEELINGS (SOME ARE POSITIVE, OTHERS NEGATIVE)
Love	Illusion, tenderness, passion, friendship, hate, …
Joy	Joy, jubilation, euphoria, sadness, nostalgia, melancholy,
Peace	Worry, affliction, tranquility, restlessness, …
Forbearance	Impatience, frustration, despair, apathy, …
Kindness	Rage, anger, interest, envy, compassion, …
Goodness	Malice, machinations, indolence, jealousy, compassion,…
Faithfulness	Betrayal, trust, distrust, hope, fear, …

Gentleness	Pride, resentment, discouragement, …
Self-Control	Shame, guilt, tension, tolerance, …

THE MANIFESTATIONS OF THE FRUIT OF THE SPIRIT OF GOD HAVE THEIR COUNTERPART IN THE EMOTIONS AND FEELINGS WE EXPERIENCE.

The list of emotions and feelings that could be included in each row of this table is endless, but one thing is clear: the manifestations of the fruit of the Spirit of God have their counterpart in the emotions and feelings we experience. Therefore, manifesting all the attributes of that fruit cannot be achieved in a week, nor in a month. This requires a lifetime.

 ## REFLECT ON A CHARACTER

In each lesson you will find two characters: a fictional one and a biblical one You can take both, or just one of them, as an example for the topic. You can also choose to read the text presented here to the group, or be inspired by it to tell your own story. This will depend on your skills and your creativity. If possible, use pictures, posters, or a projector with images. That always helps.

THE HULK

The Hulk is definitely one of the most fascinating characters in Marvel Comics!

The Hulk was a doctor and scientist who, while doing experiments with gamma rays, ended up having his genetics affected forever. We all know the result: Bruce Banner can live his life calmly and normally, but only until someone angers him. What happens then? An internal explosion. Every cell in his body begins to change, turning him into a monstrous green figure.

Do you know people like that? Or, have you ever found yourself reacting like the Hulk?

Well, emotional changes in preteens can be something like this. One moment you're at peace, and the next you're an erupting volcano.

Sometimes for a moment you are happy, and suddenly you are sad, and you do not know why. You are encouraged, and then discouraged. You are filled with enthusiasm for something, and suddenly you are disappointed.

QUESTIONS FOR THE DISCIPLES:

- Have you ever felt like the Hulk? If so, when?

- Has it happened to you that your emotions change from one moment to another? How did that make you feel?

SAUL

The first king of Israel was named Saul and we find his story in the first book of Samuel, beginning with chapter nine. Biblical history says that Saul was anointed to be king by the prophet Samuel, that he was a very tall and handsome man, and that he was honored and respected by all of God's people. He won many battles and was a good king in the first years of his reign, but there was something he couldn't shake: Saul did not think he was capable of doing what God had called him to do. He felt inferior, and that feeling led him to make several mistakes.

Although he initially had a good heart, his soul gradually changed and he began to disobey certain specific commands from God, which ultimately ended his reign. Saul was wrong to such an extent that, on one occasion, the prophet Samuel himself had to go and correct him, telling him that it was better to obey God than to sacrifice many sheep. This was said because Saul thought that making many sacrifices would make up for his disobedience.

In the latter stages of his reign, Saul already felt afflicted, overwhelmed by the condition of his soul. At a certain moment he met David, a shepherd who, with the playing of his harp, managed to calm that feeling of anguish that followed him. However, that didn't last too long either. After David defeated the giant Goliath, Saul began to develop a lot of jealousy and envy against this young warrior who had won the favor of the people. Everyone cheered for David, and Saul felt jealous and distrustful. Thus, little by little Saul lost confidence in David, and Saul's emotions led him to persecute David who, by then, had already been anointed as the new king of Israel.

Saul did not have a good ending... and in large part it was because he did not know how to handle his emotions properly.

QUESTIONS FOR THE DISCIPLES:

- What do you do when you feel jealous of someone?

- How do you handle this and your other negative emotions?

🖐 MOBILIZE

To close this first lesson, it is vital to help your preteens plan for a future in which they control their emotions. Help them make a commitment before God where they can identify those emotions that they usually cannot handle, and then decide that when that time comes, to depend on the Holy Spirit to help them control those emotions.

Give them a list of the nine manifestations of the fruit of the Holy Spirit mentioned in Galatians 5:22-23 (and it's not a bad idea to give them the printed or digital text to memorize). To conclude, ask them:

- Which of the nine manifestations of the fruit of the Spirit of God do you think you need the most for this week?

- What actions do you think you could take to make this dimension of the fruit of the Spirit more evident in your life?

Pray for them as they begin this adventure.

IDENTITY AND SELF-ESTEEM

Immature people spend more energy looking good than being better.

Lucas Leys, *Stamina*

Surely several of your preteens have seen the movie The Lion King. You can start this lesson by watching a scene or having a movie night at one of the parents' houses, or by letting one of your more outgoing preteens explain the plot of the movie to everyone. (Give them the instruction to tell it as if it were for someone who never saw it.) Another option is to read the following paragraphs to them.

When Simba was born, he was destined to be king once his father, Mufasa, stepped down from the throne. Ruling a kingdom is no easy task, but Simba, in his inexperience, thought it was something he could handle without difficulty.

However, Mufasa was killed by his own brother, Scar. And then this same evil brother drove the little heir to flee far from his territory, making Simba think that his father's death was his fault.

Simba then meets Timon and Pumba in the desert, two characters who help him overcome his remorse in exile with that famous phrase "hakuna matata." This was good for Simba in a way, as they helped him forget the sadness of the past, but along the way, they also made him forget that he was the son of the king.

As much as Simba wanted to run from the past, the essence of his being was still there inside him. Even with guilt, shame, and remorse, Simba had royal blood.

KNOWING WHO WE ARE IS KEY TO FULFILLING OUR PURPOSE ON EARTH.

He had to come back and take his rightful place in the endless circle of life! That is exactly what the baboon Rafiki reminds him of, a kind of spiritual leader who helps Simba face the past and remember who he really is.

Knowing who we are is key to fulfilling our purpose on earth. Sometimes when our identity is disrupted, our self-esteem is also affected. That is why during this lesson we will be talking about these two issues that are urgent in the preteen stage.

AVALANCHE OF IDEAS

A few years ago, it was unusual for preteens to speak out about identity or self-esteem. Today, the terms are so widespread on the internet that if you ask a preteen for their opinion on identity or self-esteem, they will surely give you a pretty accurate answer. Some of them will even give you a psychological report on their own condition, and they will define themselves as someone with high or low self-esteem. But that does not mean that they are clear on the subject.

Toss them the following statements for them to discuss if they think they are true or false, and why. (In this part you should only explore what comes to their minds when they hear these statements, without sharing your personal opinions.)

- People you admire, such as celebrities, define your identity.

- Preteens are easily influenced by their friends.

- Identity is achieved when you can look enough like someone else.

- The things that others say about you define your self-esteem.

- Parents can raise or lower their children's self-esteem.

- Healthy self-esteem does not depend on others, but on oneself.

- Someone with low self-esteem is a weak person.

Give them time to respond to each sentence before moving on to the next. It should not be a hidden or written answer, but it is good for everyone to listen to the opinions of others to see if they disagree or not with what others think.

AFTERWARDS, ALSO ASK THEM:

- What is self-esteem?

- What is identity?

- What is the relationship between those two concepts?

FOUNDATIONS OF THE THEME

Based on the "*Manual de consejería para el trabajo con adolescentes*" (*Counseling Manual for Work with Adolescents*) by e625, the construction of the identity involves three important and very well marked stages: the stage of self-discovery, the stage of formation of the life project, and the stage of the inclusion of the different spheres of life.

Identity can be defined as the construction process of a person in terms of their essence, nature, personality, vocation, and above all, character.

According to the different sciences, although there are some genetic elements that make up identity, it is a construction that each individual creates. And from the biblical point of view, it also includes the discovery of our calling and the vitality of the Creator's perspective.

The constant sensory recording of moments lived since childhood lays the foundations of what we are going to be in the future. These moments are called milestones. A milestone is that memorable memory that gives us a guideline on how to react at every moment of life.

The preteens will model their behavior based on these milestones, and will unconsciously want to obtain what they felt in them.

If these conflicts cannot be resolved from this stage to the first steps of young adulthood, a large part of their adult life will become a search to fill those deficiencies. As a discipler, you have a precious opportunity to lay firm foundations for their future. In addition, you will be able to participate in this very special stage in which the foundations of their life projects are laid. It is now, in preadolescence, as part of the construction of their identity and self-esteem, that they will consider the possibilities of the future. And you will be there to help them!

IDENTITY CAN BE DEFINED AS THE CONSTRUCTION PROCESS OF A PERSON.

Regarding self-esteem, you will have to fight together with them against various manifestations of today's society that directly affect the self-esteem of preteens. Some of the enemies of a healthy personal assessment can be: bullying, toxic relationships with close people, violence at home, parental divorce, or the hurtful and paralyzing words that preteens hear daily. The consequences of these enemies of self-esteem can vary: addictions, inappropriate sexual behavior, school dropout, rebellion, depression, etc.

Much of your work in discipling preteens will involve bringing these issues up for discussion and helping them process better. Bringing to light what affects those you disciple will be a good first step in giving them the freedom to build a healthier self-esteem, discarding those milestones that have sunk them and highlighting those that are positive.

You can start to do so by asking these questions:

- Do you know someone who is bullied, or have you ever been bullied? If so, when and where?

- Do you know what a toxic relationship is? Does something like this happen to you or has it happened to someone you know?

- Has anyone used hurtful words with you? If so, who and when? How did you feel?

Remember to be careful when asking certain questions. If the group is new and you don't feel ready to ask them, that's okay. But if you already have built trust with your preteens and can go a little further, do so, albeit cautiously.

📖 FOCUS ON TRUTH

Read with your preteens the following verses:

When Jesus came to the region of Caesarea Philippi, he asked his disciples, "Who do people say the Son of Man is?"
They replied, "Some say John the Baptist; others say Elijah; and still others, Jeremiah or one of the prophets."
"But what about you?" he asked. "Who do you say I am?"
Simon Peter answered, "You are the Messiah, the Son of the living God."
Jesus replied, "Blessed are you, Simon son of Jonah, for this was not revealed to you by flesh and blood, but by my Father in heaven.
Matthew 16:13-17

This portion of Scripture shows Jesus discussing his identity and what people were saying about him. They gave him some options, but Jesus really didn't care what other people said about him, but only what his closest friends said of him. That is why he asked the same question to them again:

"Who do you say I am?"

For Peter, this conversation was not only important, it was defining. Peter's affirmation that Jesus was the Messiah, the Son of the living God, the Christ, gave him a powerful "spiritual moment." "God has blessed you," Jesus told him, and he recognized that this revelation did not come from human wisdom, but from God himself. Look how the text continues:

> "And I tell you that you are Peter, and on this *rock I will build my church, and the gates of Hades will not overcome it. I will give you the keys of the kingdom of heaven; whatever you bind on earth will be bound in heaven, and whatever you loose on earth will be loosed in heaven.*"
> **Matthew 16:18–19**

So, being clear about the identity of Jesus changed Peter's life forever and reaffirmed the reason why Jesus had changed his name, giving meaning to his spiritual identity. The same can happen with us!

When we clarify the identity of Jesus, we also clarify our own.

WHEN WE CLARIFY THE IDENTITY OF JESUS, WE ALSO CLARIFY OUR OWN.

Furthermore, each of us would do well to repeat this reflective conversation in our own lives. Many times, we pay too much attention to the opinions of other people, such as schoolmates and other circumstantial companions, but we forget that only the closest people are important in this sense. Those with whom we have opened up enough to know the depths of our hearts are the ones who can best comment on our identity. That is why it is vital to choose wisely who these people will be, in addition to those who are part of our family.

Disciplers should be able to access that level with our preteens! They should listen to what we have to say about them because, thanks to the relationship we are building, we can tell them how we see them for who they really are, despite what the world tells them.

Now let's read this passage of Scripture that teaches us about the relationship between God's love and our identity:

See what great love the Father has lavished on us, that we should be called children of God! And that is what we are! The reason the world does not know us is that it did not know him.

1 John 3:1

Thanks to his infinite love we can call ourselves children of God! The condition of children makes us part of a family of which God is the Father, and therefore he is the one who can best assign us identity.

OUR BIGGEST CHALLENGE IN THE CONSTRUCTION OF OUR IDENTITY IS BEING ABLE TO SEE OURSELVES AS HE SEES US.

DETAILS TO TEACH PRETEENS:

- Let's pay attention to verse 2 when it says that we cannot imagine what we are going to be like after death, but what we must be sure of is that we will be similar to him.

- Our biggest challenge in the construction of our identity is being able to see ourselves as he sees us

- The more we look at Christ, who is the image of the Father, the more we will see the Father; and the more we see him, the more we know about him, and consequently, the more like him we will be.

- The Father does not look at us based on what we are today, but on the design that he put in us; he looks at us based on our purpose and sees us fulfilling our destiny.

- As we move towards our destiny, we are being perfected, and every day we have more information about what God wants for us.

Knowing all this is key to building identity! Knowing what the Lord thinks of us raises our self-esteem. On the contrary, listening to what the devil says against us causes us to lose ourselves in guilt and shame, and makes us feel incapable of being what God says we are.

INTROSPECTION

This is the time to help your preteens reflect on what's on their mind with the following questions:

- Who is helping you form your identity, even if they don't know they're doing it?

- What qualities of your personality would you like to stand out, that everyone can recognize in you?

- What should you do today to start building the future you want?

- What positive things do you already have to help you achieve that future?

- Who would you like to help and to accompany you to discover and form your identity in Christ?

 REFLECT ON A CHARACTER

Choose one or both of the following characters and tell their story to your preteens. Or, if the group knows them, let them tell you about the characters. It also helps to show them a summary video, or a shocking scene, and then move on to the questions.

MULAN

Mulan is the daughter of a retired warrior, who had served his country for many years and who, in a moment of conflict, is called back to join the forces of the Chinese army, an institution in which only men were allowed to participate. For that warrior, age did not matter, nor did his war injuries; far greater to him were the principles he had learned from childhood, and which had taken root in his heart. He would go to the battlefield at any cost. He would answer the call without hesitation.

Worried about her father, and trying to defend him from this sacrifice, Mulan decides to pose as his son in order to be able to replace her father in the call for war, without considering that with this action, she would dishonor her family by going against the culture of the nation.

Infiltrated in the army, surrounded by men, struggling with not really being a warrior, and in fear of discovery, Mulan never lost sight of the purpose for which she was there. She would never let her father be the one to uselessly sacrifice himself. She would fight, she would become a warrior, and she would do whatever it took to save him.

Mulan's story is a recognition of those who decide to defend their principles even at the cost of their own lives, amid a culture that would judge and condemn their actions. Starting with Mulan, the Chinese people looked at women differently, and although it took them decades to fight against such traditions, this fact became a milestone that transformed the entire culture.

QUESTIONS FOR THE DISCIPLES:

- What positive attitudes can we take from the story of Mulan?

- What would happen to the world if we, the children of God, infiltrated it to defend our Father's principles?

- Would we be able to maintain our identity, or would we let ourselves be carried away by what the world says? Why do you think that would happen?

JOHN, THE APOSTLE

Here we are talking about nothing more and nothing less than the writer of the most intimate gospel of the Bible, and also the one to whom the book of Revelation was given. But it is not only those books of the Bible that allow us to know this apostle in depth but, above all, his pastoral letters.

John wrote in a very intimate way. His gospel is called "the gospel of love" surely because the author's intention was to make known to the world the supernatural love that he had experienced while being close to Jesus. On the other hand, some see the messages to the churches narrated in the first chapters of the book of Revelation as rigid warnings from a God who brings justice. However, when reading John's writings, we see that he did not speak tragically, but rather about God's protection and deep concern for human beings.

When John begins his letters, he calls his disciples "little children." Such endearing affection is not only a personality quality, but is clear evidence of having received that same affection from the eternal Father. John considers the fact of being called children by God as a great sign of love. John was sure of who he was in Christ, and knowing God deeply through Jesus allowed him to speak as he did.

QUESTIONS FOR THE DISCIPLES:

- Could you say similar things to what John said? Why or why not?

- In what ways is John worthy of imitation?

MOBILIZE

A large part of the work of a discipler consists of getting involved in the lives of those whom you are discipling, contacting their family, and creating some casual encounters and other intentional spaces where you can go deeper in the process of accompaniment.

Remember that it is very possible that any specific action you take in this process will become a milestone: a memorable memory that will serve as a reference in the life of that boy or girl. They will remember it forever, and many of their future actions will be influenced by that memory.

What milestones can you create in your relationship with your preteens?

HERE ARE SOME IDEAS:

- **A special letter.** Arrange ahead of time for the parents (or someone close to them) to write them a letter highlighting everything positive and important about them, and have them include a blessing or wish on them as well. Then all the boys and girls will open their letters at a special moment in a meeting or activity, like you would do at a camp.

- **Public recognition.** Create a space within services or preteen meetings, to recognize the positive things that each boy or girl has. Highlight their successes, their talents, thank them for their good deeds, and give them the impetus to keep going. If you focus on one or two of them each week, throughout the year you can reach all your preteens.

- **Self-esteem meeting.** Organize a meeting for preteens to say positive things to each other, mainly about the future. It will be better if you do it in a small group. Give everyone the task of imagining what every other boy and girl will be like in 5 or 10 years. Warn them not to see negative things but positive ones: professional successes, use of their talents, healthy personal relationships, etc.

- **Visit their home.** You can schedule a visit to talk with their parents and tell them all the positive things you see in their child. Focus on the talents and abilities that you see in them. Be on the lookout if either parent tries to use this time to complain about their son's or daughter's behavior. You must be very skillful and wise to turn the complaint into a possibility of positive change for the future.

Remember that this material is not designed to be rushed to complete a curriculum, but you can extend it as much as you want. You could use a week for each topic, or up to a month if you wanted. From one lesson you may want to branch out to several sessions, using different activities and topics to complete a deeper process in the development of those under your care.

LESSON 3

FACING MY FEARS

I prefer to surround myself with people who reveal their imperfection, rather than people who fake their perfection.

Charles F. Glassman, *Brain Drain*

We all experience anxieties and fears. Fear is real regardless of its reasons and even when its reasons are only in our mind. We start with this statement because one of the worst fears of many Christians is expressing that they feel anxiety or fear. In essence, we are afraid of fear, which happens to us not only with this emotion but even with sadness, and proof of that is how quickly we tell someone who has lost a family member that "God uses all things for good" so that they no longer feel sad. Fear is natural and even positive because it emerges from our instinct for self-preservation and love for life. It is even an expression of the love we have for others. When it becomes negative is when it takes control of us and governs our emotions, or worse, when it influences our decisions, and that's why it's vital to talk about this theme with preteens.

AVALANCHE OF IDEAS

Materials for the introductory activity:

- Enough blindfolds or handkerchiefs to blindfold all participants.

- A series of things with different textures that feel scary, but are actually harmless. For example, something sticky (like slime), something very hairy (like a stuffed animal, and if it's one that moves, even better), a dry branch that does not break, a little shampoo, yogurt, sand, powder, etc. (Maybe you can also get a small frog or turtle in a fish tank.) The more things you have, the better.

- A feather or something similar.

For this activity you will also need an accomplice, who can be a support leader or, if there is no one else, one of the preteens (choose the one who is more mature and knows how to follow rules and explain the activity to them beforehand).

When you have blindfolded everyone, tell them that you have brought some items and they will have to guess if they are inanimate objects, animals, or plants. If you want a more intense experience, play forest, jungle, or animal music on your cell phone. You can even tell a whole story while explaining the game to them. Tell them, for example, that you have brought some pets that you have borrowed, some small, and others not so much. Whether the activity is really intense or not will depend on the story you tell!

Then you are going to bring each of the preteens, blindfolded, to the table where the chosen objects are. You will give them some objects to touch, and they will have to guess in each case if it is an inanimate object, or an animal, or a plant. But to make it more interesting, you won't give them all the same objects, nor in the same order, but you will rotate them to mislead them. While all this is going on, your accomplice will take the feather and hold it close to the kids' ears to increase the tension.

Like we said, how "scary" this activity is will depend on the story you tell them and the items you get. To the list that we already mentioned, you could add toy spiders or similar things, but the expectation of fear will be generated by the environment you create.

Obviously, some of the boys and girls will be completely calm, others will struggle to show that they are in control of their emotions, and others will scream in fear!

Hardly anyone will be able to guess what each one touched, so in the end let them see with their eyes uncovered all the items. Then have a little chat with them so they can tell you how they felt while they were blindfolded. Not everyone will have felt fear, but they will be able to report different sensations that resemble fear.

That is how you will open today's lesson!

Note: If you've organized a virtual meeting, you can have the same effect by showing kids images of things that might scare them (without traumatizing them, of course). Ask them to comment in the group on the sensation that each of the images produced in them, and to identify the situation that frightens them the most. The experience will not be the same, but it will point to the same purpose.

FOUNDATIONS OF THE THEME

Fear is an intense emotion that allows us to react to some danger or threat. A barking dog can cause us a certain level of fear, enough to cross to the sidewalk in front of us, but if we were to meet a tiger, we would surely feel much more afraid. Probably so much that we would run at the maximum possible speed! This happens with situations of real danger, but it can also happen with imaginary situations and therein lies one of the fundamental aspects: we must learn to control fear so that it does not control us.

So, if fear itself is not bad, since it helps us protect ourselves and wards off danger, what is the problem? The problem is that when it grows too much, or when it arises due to unreal things, it is a barrier that prevents us from moving forward. That is the fear we must overcome.

In order to overcome it, we must first understand that fear moves in cycles. It originates with a bad experience that we do not want to repeat. The fear of repeating that experience later produces an inability to react appropriately. That inability causes us to have a bad experience again, and thus the cycle repeats itself.

This is what the cycle of fear looks like:

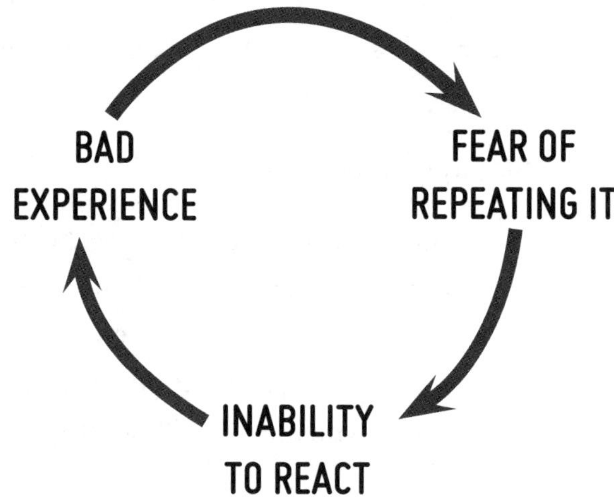

For example:

- A person throws a child into the pool to learn to swim.

- The child cannot swim, and almost drowns.

- The child does not want to repeat that experience again, and that is why they are afraid of the water.

- Even when they are older, they cannot learn to swim, or at least it is very difficult for them.

- Every time they enter a pool, that fear will return.

Understanding this cycle of fear makes us see how important it is to discuss the issue with our children. Many of the attitudes that adults have are caused by some type of fear that they feel and that they have not been able to resolve, and this shapes their behavior, preventing them from being free. The fear, then, becomes a prison that keeps the person incarcerated for their entire life and does not allow them to be what they have been called to be.

Steps to facing fears:

- Identify the fear.

- Explore the moment when it appeared in your life.

- Remember how you reacted in that moment.

- Understand the parts of that fear that exist only in your mind.

- Go to the Word of God to put faith in the Lord as the real foundation of your confidence and security.

- Take concrete steps to free yourself from fear.

Once you have identified what fear you want to face, you must remember when and under what circumstances it appeared in your life. Observe the feelings that scene still causes in you when you remember it. When seeking to understand which factors are only in your mind, try to have objective judgment. In the swimming example, the factor only in the mind would be thinking that you could drown in a pool where you can stand on the bottom and have your head above the water with no problem. In this way you can clearly verify that your fear is not real. Then you must go to God and ask for strength, courage, and protection, to face that fear and be free from it. You will take small steps at first, until little by little you will free yourself!

📖 FOCUS ON TRUTH

But the Lord God called to the man, "Where are you?"
He answered, "I heard you in the garden,
and I was afraid because I was naked; so I hid.
Genesis 3:9–10

We were created to stay connected to God. In the garden of Eden there was a perfect union, and spiritual communication with the Creator was unimpeded.

IN THE GARDEN OF EDEN THERE WAS A PERFECT UNION WITH THE CREATOR. THE FIRST MISTAKE OF THE HUMAN BEING CAUSED US TO LOSE THAT CONNECTION.

The first mistake (or sin) of the human being caused us to lose that connection. Our spirit experienced the condition of death, and our soul began to take control of us, affecting the body and our entire being. There fear appeared, in a negative context.

Observe the following comparison.

Condition before sin:

- They were not afraid

- They were naked and unashamed.

- They spoke directly to God.

- Adam and Eve had a perfect relationship together.

Condition after sin:

- Hey began to fear God and have other fears.

- God had to cover them for their shame.

- They hid from God and stopped listening to him.

- Adam and Eve began to blame each other for their mistakes.

Let us now review another portion of Scripture, comparing 2 Timothy 1:7 in different versions:

1. "For the Spirit God gave us does not make us timid, but gives us power, love and self-discipline." (New International Version)

2. "For God has not given us a spirit of fear, but of power and of love and of a sound mind." (New King James Version)

3. "For God has not given us a spirit of fear and timidity, but of power, love, and self-discipline. " (New Living Translation)

4. "For God gave us not a spirit of fearfulness; but of power and love and discipline." (American Standard Version)

It is interesting to observe the different words that the Bible uses as synonyms for fear, such as timidity. It is likely that even if some of your preteens have not always felt fear, they have felt timid at some point in their lives.

In either case, it is important that those you are discipling know that God has given them a spirit that can overcome fear, since he is a spirit full of supernatural and divine strength, love, and self-control. Remind them that usually, when fear invades us, it is because our minds are deceived to think things contrary to what God has told us.

WHEN FEAR INVADES US, IT IS BECAUSE OUR MINDS ARE DECEIVED TO THINK THINGS CONTRARY TO WHAT GOD HAS TOLD US.

Another classic story that talks about facing fear is that of Peter getting out of the boat when Jesus called him to walk on the water.

Immediately Jesus made the disciples get into the boat and go on ahead of him to the other side, while he dismissed the crowd. After he had dismissed them, he went up on a mountainside by himself to pray. Later that night, he was there alone, and the boat was already a considerable distance from land, buffeted by the waves because the wind was against it.

Shortly before dawn Jesus went out to them, walking on the lake. When the disciples saw him walking on the lake, they were terrified. "It's a ghost," they said, and cried out in fear.
But Jesus immediately said to them: "Take courage! It is I. Don't be afraid."
"Lord, if it's you," Peter replied, "tell me to come to you on the water."
"Come," he said.
Then Peter got down out of the boat, walked on the water and came toward Jesus. But when he saw the wind, he was afraid and, beginning to sink, cried out, "Lord, save me!"
Immediately Jesus reached out his hand and caught him. "You of little faith," he said, "why did you doubt?"
And when they climbed into the boat, the wind died down. Then those who were in the boat worshiped him, saying, "Truly you are the Son of God."
Matthew 14:22–33

When Jesus started walking towards the disciples early in the morning, the scene was so strange they thought it was a ghost, but Jesus told them it was him and to not be afraid. Peter then told him that if it really was the Master, he would order him to walk to where he was. Jesus did so, and Peter began to walk on the water... until he realized what he was doing and saw how huge the waves were all around him and he started sinking.

A PERSON CAN HAVE DOUBTS ABOUT DIFFERENT ASPECTS OF THE BIBLE. BUT YOU CAN'T DOUBT THE POWER OF GOD!

Many times, when we have an unfounded fear, it has to do with the fact that we doubt the power of God. A person can have doubts about different aspects of the Bible, doubts about historical issues or interpretations, but you can't doubt the power of God! If you are a disciple, if you trust in God, you cannot doubt his power to accomplish everything he said he was going to accomplish!

🛠 INTROSPECTION

Present the following list of fears to your preteens, and ask them to check off those that they feel have affected their lives:

- Public Speaking _______

- Heights _______

- Being alone _______

- Looking bad or doing something embarrassing _______

- Water or swimming _______

- Death of a loved one _______

- The future _______

- Failure _______

- Dying _______

- Sickness _______

- Being a nobody _______

- Not having friends _______

- Other people's criticism _______

Then, open the conversation for someone to share with the group a personal experience of fear. Or ask your boys and girls to share what their biggest fear is. (It could be one that is on the list, or it could be something new.) There are times that are more lighthearted, but these moments are to open the heart, and no one should make fun of the others even if they don't understand what they feel or why they say what they say. Teach them to be respectful in sharing times.

To close out this part, teach your preteens these four powerful biblical concepts:

1. **Truth defeats fear.**

   To the Jews who had believed him, Jesus said "If you hold to my teaching, you are really my disciples. Then you will know the truth, and the truth will set you free." **(John 8:31–32)**

   Knowing the truth, which is Jesus, allows us to be free from many things, including fear. If we do not know the truth of God expressed through Christ, we will remain in fear.

2. **Love defeats fear.**

   There is no fear in love. But perfect love drives out fear, because fear has to do with punishment. The one who fears is not made perfect in love. **(1 John 4:18)**

   If the perfect love that comes from God is real, then we know that fear will be cast out, because God is love. If God is in us, there is no room for fear.

3. **Faith defeats fear.**

   And without faith it is impossible to please God, because anyone who comes to him must believe that he exists and that he rewards those who earnestly seek him. **(Hebrews 11:6)**

   Without faith it is impossible to please God; therefore, fear can be a manifestation of lack of faith, or disbelief. Developing our faith and putting it into practice enables to us overcome all fear!

4. **Courage defeats fear.**

   Have I not commanded you? Be strong and courageous. Do not be afraid; do not be discouraged, for the Lord your God will be with you wherever you go. **(Joshua 1:9)**

God has already ordered it: we must not be afraid or let circumstances discourage us. The Lord commands us to be strong and courageous!

 REFLECT ON A CHARACTER

DAREDEVIL

He is known in the world of comics as "the man without fear". Daredevil is a blind lawyer who practices his profession in *Hell's Kitchen*, a city that represents troubled New York, where the mafia and gangsters run everything, including the police.

He lost his sight as a child, and around the same time lost his father to being involved with the mob. Thus, he grew up prodigiously developing some extraordinary abilities to compensate for his lack of sight.

He has his red suit, and he is skilled in street fighting. A blind man? Yes, a blind man who developed superhuman abilities. But the greatest capacity of all that he possesses is that he is not afraid.

The story of this character reflects the way in which we can face the circumstances of life. For him, the only way to face life is without fear!

QUESTIONS FOR THE DISCIPLES:

- Do you think that if a person is excessively afraid of something, they can overcome it? Why or why not?

- Can you live without fear? Do you think this would be good? Why or why not?

PETER

The Bible hides nothing, and it has not been a problem for any of the biblical writers to describe in full detail what really happened. This is another of the arguments that gives evidence that the Word of God is a reliable and true instrument.

It is said that Peter was very close to Jesus. From the day his spiritual eyes were opened, and he became certain that Jesus was the Christ, everything in Peter's life changed. Peter had been an impetuous and strong fisherman, capable of shouldering all the hard work that his trade required. Because of that same strong character, Peter was the one who asked the questions that the others did not dare to ask, and he had more initiative than the rest of his friends. All of that was positive, but he also had to deal with aspects of his character that he couldn't seem to control. Peter was impulsive, to the point that in a fit of anger he decided to cut off the ear of one of those who wanted to arrest his Master! Jesus had to counter Peter's abrupt reaction by performing a miracle and putting the ear back in place.

Despite being so strong and impetuous there was an occasion when Peter had to face fear, and fear overcame him. We refer to the moment that we read about a few pages ago, in which Jesus walked on the water and called Peter to do the same. Peter was an experienced fisherman, and he knew what it meant to get out of the boat in the middle of troubled waters: he would inevitably sink. At first, he decided to overcome his fear of the storm and trust in Jesus, and this allowed him to walk a few steps in victory. But then he doubted, and that doubt caused him to begin to sink.

QUESTIONS FOR THE DISCIPLES:

- Can you remember a time in your own life when trust in God helped you overcome fear? When was it and what happened?

- Can you remember a time in your own life when doubt or a lack of trust in God caused you to sink? When was it and what happened?

- What should we imitate from Peter and what should we not?

MOBILIZE

Write down and give these four powerful Biblical concepts to your preteens:

1. **Truth defeats fear.**

   To the Jews who had believed him, Jesus said, "If you hold to my teaching, you are really my disciples. Then you will know the truth, and the truth will set you free." **(John 8:31–32)**

2. **Love defeats fear.**

   There is no fear in love. But perfect love drives out fear, because fear has to do with punishment. The one who fears is not made perfect in love. **(1 John 4:18)**

3. **Faith defeats fear.**

   And without faith it is impossible to please God, because anyone who comes to him must believe that he exists and that he rewards those who earnestly seek him. **(Hebrews 11:6)**

4. **Courage defeats fear.**

   Be strong and courageous. Do not be afraid; do not be discouraged, for the Lord your God will be with you wherever you go. **(Joshua 1:9)**

Be sure they know how to use the weapon of the Word of God in each step of their walk as disciples. It will be a great help to live full lives and free from unnecessary fears.

It's time to face our fears!

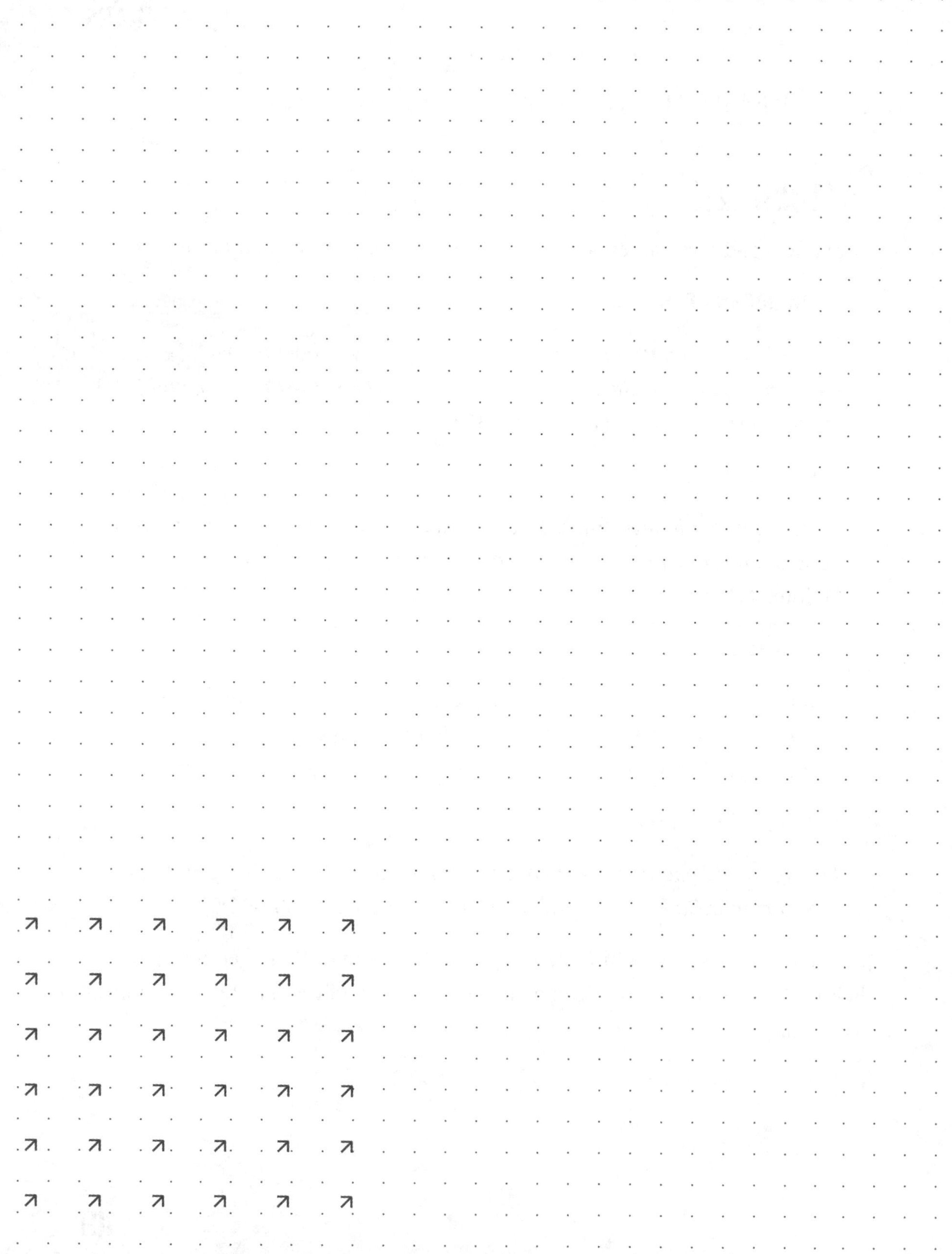

LESSON 4

THE CRISIS OF SHAME

People who feel guilt and shame often walk with stooped shoulders, their heads hanging. They convey the appearance that they want to hide.

Don Colbert, *Deadly Emotions*

In the same way as many kids feel confident in everything because of their lack of experience, preteens often find themselves on the other side, experiencing a lot of shame. If they've already found out they're not good at sports or singing or school, they're probably terrified that other preteens will find out. Around this time they often start to build up some insecurities; it's important to get over these as soon as possible.

 AVALANCHE OF IDEAS

CRAZY PAINTING

In this activity everyone is going to paint their faces. Tell your boys and girls to ask for permission and bring makeup that their mom uses or get face paint in different colors (many party supply stores have these). Also remember to bring makeup removal lotion so you can remove their makeup/face paint later.

Prepare the group by warning them that they are going to laugh a little, because they are going to paint themselves in an exaggerated way until they look very funny. The idea is for them to try to look as if they were adults. You will tell the girls to put blush on their cheeks and a lot of eye shadow on their eyes. The idea is not that they look beautiful, but rather humorous. You will tell the boys to draw mustaches and beards. If someone wants to go further and paint themselves as a clown or as an animal, that is also allowed.

While they do, make sure you are there watching. Do not let the situation get out of control, because sometimes preteens are a bit cruel since they still do not know how to handle the way they express themselves, and they can end up hurting others without meaning to. Therefore, you must be attentive to shape their behavior. They need to learn to respect others and not hurt other kids' feelings, and it will be better if they hear it from someone with strong Christian values. This is also part of discipleship!

When they are ready, ask everyone to introduce themselves. What adult character did they choose to be? It can be one of their parents, or their future selves. It could even be a celebrity actor or actress, or a famous YouTuber.

As they introduce themselves, you can ask them questions to make it more fluid and fun. Little by little, the embarrassment they may have will dissipate between laughter, and the discomfort will fade away. Then you can start the topic.

If you're in a virtual meeting, another alternative to this activity is for everyone to share an embarrassing memory they have.

As always, remember that sharing times are optional, not required. Although we want kids to talk about what they feel inside, we can't, and shouldn't, force them if they don't want to.

📝 FOUNDATIONS OF THE THEME

Shame is one of those emotions that can haunt us from when we are children until we are adults, or even when we are elderly. Nobody is safe from going through moments of shame, because life often puts us in situations that can embarrass us. It will be a challenge for you as a discipler to gain the confidence of your preteens to be able to enter into increasingly complex and intimate topics, since talking about what makes them feel uncomfortable is not an easy task. Especially at these ages, in which some things such as clothing, looking good in front of others, and feeling accepted are so important. While the boys and girls continue on this journey, they must face countless situations in which they will feel insecure, ashamed, or embarrassed. Your duty is to accompany them in this process, listen to them with love, and guide them in this journey in such a way that the most insecure aspects of their behavior are affirmed, and they no longer feel that every uncomfortable situation they experience is the worst disaster of their lives.

> **MANY ADULTS CONSIDER PROBLEMS IN THEIR RELATIONSHIPS, WORK, ETC. TO POINT TO THE ISSUES THEY FAILED TO SUCCESSFULLY OVERCOME IN THE EARLIER STAGES OF LIFE.**

Warning: Our job as disciplers is not to tell preteens how to dress, or how to act, because that would take away part of their identity. Rather, what we should do is give them positive parameters, and be available to them when they feel that something did not go as they would have wanted.

WHY IS IT IMPORTANT TO ADDRESS THE ISSUE OF SHAME?

Something that happens a lot with preteens is that they hold on to certain feelings that can affect them in the future. In fact, many adults consider problems in their relationships, work, etc. to point to the issues they failed to successfully overcome in the earlier stages of life.

In addition, since bullying is so present today, it is important to give our boys and girls the tools to defend themselves (in a good way) from these types of social attacks.

Some situations that can cause shame in this stage are:

- **Not meeting social expectations.** A conversation with someone of the opposite sex, an invitation that didn't come through, not fitting in or not feeling part of a group, feeling that others are talking behind their backs, etc., are things that cause insecurity and shame in boys and girls of this age.

- **Bullying and other forms of harassment.** This is one of the situations that produce the greatest shame among preteens and teens. Being disturbed by someone who denigrates your integrity on any level is not a light thing.

- **Change of physical appearance, tone of voice, etc.** All the changes that puberty brings can be reasons to feel insecure, watched, and affected. To make matters worse, it's likely that at every meeting you go to, you'll run into people who, in an attempt to praise someone else, may point out something they're probably trying to hide in order to go unnoticed.

- **An embarrassing experience.** A fall in front of everyone, an unplanned burp, flatulence, accidentally torn or wet pants, or anything that exposes them in front of others are all experienced with great anguish by preteens.

"The adolescent's fear of ridicule and the need for social acceptance collide head-on with the anguish of an unattractive body image, which contrasts unfavorably with the stereotypes of masculine and feminine beauty disseminated by society and the media". *Pedagogía y Psicología Infantil: Pubertad y adolescencia [Pedagogy and Child Psychology: Puberty and adolescence]*

HOW DOES A PRETEEN HANDLE SHAME?

Human beings are multifaceted. This means that there are many factors that influence our behavior, and therefore it is almost unpredictable how a preteen may react in each case. The temperament of each boy or girl also influences behavior. Someone introverted will probably feel withdrawn, and it won't be easy for them to talk about it when they're embarrassed. For someone extroverted, on the other hand, the solution may be to laugh at themselves, and thus they can overcome an embarrassing situation without problem.

Your ability as a discipler must be in discerning these factors, so that you can accompany each preteen in a more personal way. It will also be key that you use empathy. Put yourself in the shoes of each of your boys and girls to better think about how to help them carry the load.

📖 FOCUS ON TRUTH

Remember that if you want to do more in-depth discipleship work and spend more time on each topic, you can take one, two, or even four weeks for each lesson. In some lessons there may be too much material to cover in a single week. It is up to you and the evaluation you make of the needs of your particular group.

On this occasion, in our study of the Word of God we will be talking about Jesus, the one who bore all our shame. But before this, we will talk about when shame appeared in the world. Do you know when it was? Yes, of course you do. It started with Adam and Eve.

Let's see the difference.

Adam and his wife were both naked, and they felt no shame.
Genesis 2:25

Here we see that before sinning, Adam and Eve were naked but didn't feel shame.

At that moment their eyes were opened, and they suddenly felt shame at their nakedness. So they sewed fig leaves together to cover themselves.
Genesis 3:7 (NLT)

We notice that after they sinned they were ashamed, they hid from God, and they had to find leaves to cover themselves.

SHAME WAS A CONSEQUENCE OF SIN.

That's when shame appeared! And yes, it was a consequence of sin! Therefore, every time we disobey God we have that kind of desire to hide, just like Adam and Eve did. (As you can see, shame is tied to fear, the theme we dealt with in the previous lesson.) From there, shame spread throughout the world, and today it is one of the tools the enemy uses the most to stop us. If he manages to make us feel ashamed, then he knows that this will limit us and prevent us from fulfilling God's purpose in our lives!

Now, read with your preteens the following passage:

You have made us a reproach to our neighbors, the scorn and derision of those around us. You have made us a byword among the nations; the peoples shake their heads at us. I live in disgrace all day long, and my face is covered with shame at the taunts of those who reproach and revile me, because of the enemy, who is bent on revenge.
Psalms 44:13–16

This passage is impressive, isn't it? It tells us about a series of calamities that the people of Israel had to go through at a certain stage in their history. Sure, this was for disobedience, but they complained to God as if he were to blame for the bad things that happened to them. God was not to blame; it was actually their own fault because of the hardness of their hearts and their constant rebellion against God. But notice how, at this stage, the people received humiliation and ridicule from other nations.

Maybe that's when bullying was invented! We also see how this whole series of altered emotions made them blame God. But it was not the right attitude. If they had only surrendered, repented, and asked for forgiveness, God would have saved them without hesitation. They would not have been ridiculed; they would not have been a laughingstock for everyone.

IF JESUS COULD TAKE ALL THE SHAME UPON HIMSELF, THEN WE CAN LOOK TO HIM TO FREE US OF ALL SHAME.

There are many other passages of Scripture that talk about shame, but now we want to focus on Jesus. He was the one who took our shame upon himself, as we read in the next verse:

> *Fixing our eyes on Jesus, the pioneer and perfecter of faith. For the joy set before him he endured the cross, scorning its shame, and sat down at the right hand of the throne of God.*
> **Hebrews 12:2**

The way Jesus died was humiliating. Naked, insulted, despised, and degraded to the worst punishment, to the worst form of torture that existed at that time to end the life of a person... and all so that we can achieve peace and redemption (Isaiah 53:4-9). He kept silent because he knew that he had to obey the Father, and that with this act he would save all humanity.

Today we are part of that humanity that has been rescued from the punishment of death and the shame of the world, to be welcomed into the kingdom of the Son of God! (Colossians 1:13)

Explain this to your preteens: If Jesus could take all the shame upon himself, and rise from the grave in victory, then we can look to him to free us of all shame and help us overcome those feelings of embarrassment that could haunt us.

Jesus took all the shame on our behalf!

⚙ INTROSPECTION

Ask your preteens to read the following sentences carefully and then say, for each one, if they think it is true or false.

- When there is something that embarrasses me, I must hide it so that no one finds out.______

- Shame will haunt me forever. ______

- The feeling of shame can be defeated thanks to Jesus. ______

- Shame is not important; I shouldn't listen to it. ______

- Shame for something that happened to us by accident is different from shame for something we did on purpose. ______

(You can add to the list other statements that you consider important to help your boys and girls reflect).

As a discipler, you must be attentive to the responses of each of the participants. Some of these phrases can be misleading, so make the most of each answer. It may also happen that some of their answers are as simple as "yes" or "no"; in those cases you should bring out your skills as a discipler. Preteens often tend to respond with monosyllables, but you should ask them for their opinions and teach them to think through more complex sentences.

 # REFLECT ON A CHARACTER

HICCUP, THE DRAGON TRAINER

DreamWorks produced the animated film *How to Train Your Dragon* based on the books by Cressida Cowell. Its main character is Hiccup, a teenager from the Viking town who had grown up full of complexities. Since childhood he had felt different from others. Everyone in his town was strong and brave but Hiccup felt like a weakling. When they were all trained to hunt dragons, he did not want to do it, because he felt compassion for them.

That feeling of not fitting in, coupled with his father's constant disapproving gestures, had confined him to a prison of shame. Hiccup was insecure, like many boys his age nowadays, and didn't have the confidence to speak up about this with his father or anyone else. Even later, when he was able to tame a one-of-a-kind dragon, Hiccup still didn't feel like he was someone fit to be considered a true Viking.

Being the laughingstock of the town brought a great shame to Hiccup's heart that made him unable to face life's problems. He suffered because of who he was and how others saw him. Fortunately, throughout the film we can see his process of abandoning shame and insecurity, to become what he had been called to be.

By the end of the film we can see how little by little he is taking risks to save all his people, including his father, from an evil dragon that controlled the rest of the dragons. Hiccup grew up to be courageous, capable of facing the fiercest of all enemies with intelligence and wit, and he was able to do what no other Viking could have done with their muscles and physical strength!

QUESTIONS FOR THE DISCIPLES:

- In what circumstances today can we feel like Hiccup?

- What did Hiccup do to get over his shame.

JOHN THE BAPTIST

Jesus knew John from before he was born, when they were both in their mothers' wombs. Although Scripture does not mention much about his childhood and adolescence, it is very likely that, as the son of Mary's cousin, John was someone very close to Jesus in his childhood years. Already having reached young adulthood, John reappears in the Bible and a brief but rather striking description is made of him. You can find it in the story of Jesus's baptism in the Gospels of Matthew, Mark, and Luke.

Here is Matthew's version:

In those days John the Baptist came, preaching in the wilderness of Judea and saying, "Repent, for the kingdom of heaven has come near." This is he who was spoken of through the prophet Isaiah:
"A voice of one calling in the wilderness, 'Prepare the way for the Lord, make straight paths for him.'
John's clothes were made of camel's hair, and he had a leather belt around his waist. His food was locusts and wild honey. People went out to him from Jerusalem and all Judea and the whole region of the Jordan. Confessing their sins, they were baptized by him in the Jordan River.
Matthew 3:1–6

John was a traveling preacher, and his biggest stage was the desert. His clothes were made of camel hair, and his food was wild honey and lobsters (not the marine crustacean, but huge crickets). From this brief description we can realize that he was a person that others would consider "strange." His clothes and his food were not something common in his time, nor was his way of living in the deserted like a hermit. His preaching was harsh, but nevertheless John led many to repent and turn to God. Thus, it was necessary for it to happen, since this man came to prepare the way for the arrival of the Messiah.

It is interesting to note that John did not seem to care about his image or what others might think of him. John cared more about his purpose, that for which he had been called by God. Most likely, a lot of people were talking bad about him behind his back, but that didn't stop him at all! John was so committed to his call that he decided to ignore any of the strategies the enemy used to try to stop him.

The example of John the Baptist is powerful. He did not seek the approval of men. More important than what he wore or what he ate was what he had come to do for the kingdom of God. He avoided being overcome by shame because he considered his calling more valuable than what others could say about him.

QUESTIONS FOR THE DISCIPLES:

- Have you felt ashamed of the way you dress or what you do? If so, when?

- Have you felt that your image is more important than your purpose? If so, when?

- What example can we take from John the Baptist in this regard?

MOBILIZE

Here's a helpful step-by-step guide to share with your preteens.

If I have committed a sin that embarrasses me, what should I do?

- Ask for forgiveness before anything else. That means, first, getting right with God for that fault, with the certainty that God always forgives us. There is nothing, however embarrassing it may be, that God cannot forgive!

- Genuinely repent. To repent is to change your mind on the subject. If before you thought it was okay to do this or that, to truly repent is to wish not to do it again, realizing that it caused hurt.

- Receive cleansing. God cleanses us from all sin when we follow these steps, but it is up to us to feel that cleansing and believe that it is true. We cannot continue to feel guilty for something we did when we have already asked for forgiveness. You must receive that forgiveness and know that God is faithful to his promise.

If others embarrassed me, what should I do?

- Forgive. Pray for the person who offended you, asking for a blessing for this person, and asking God to put peace and forgiveness in your heart.

- Deal with feelings. Think of a way to bless or do good to the person who embarrassed you. This will transform your feelings. You can highlight something you like about him or her, write him or her a message, or comment positively on a post on social media, etc.

- Get rid of the guilt. Find verses that talk about who you are to God. Stick them on your mirror, or on the wall next to your bed, and repeat them every night.

- Tell someone. Find a friend, a leader, or someone you trust, and tell them what happened to you. This will give you a better perspective than what you repeat over and over in your own head.

- Analyze the severity of the issue. Sometimes the abuser can do it deceitfully, and can even make you feel good things at times. It may also be that the abuser asks you to keep it a secret, or threatens you with things that scare you. That is why it is difficult for you to stop the abuse. How do you know how bad it is? Without a doubt, it is serious, and you should ask for help if any of the following situations occur:

1. The person who offends you threatens you with worse consequences if you tell someone.

2. The offense threatens your physical health, or if there are blows that leave bruises, cuts, or cause pain for more than a while.

3. The offense has to do with your sexuality: kisses on the mouth, caresses on your genitals, or on their genitals, and/or makes you see sexual images.

4. Being close to someone who offends you is very scary; you feel like hiding or running away.

5. The person who offends you forces you to send them naked photos, or sends you photos of their private parts, and threatens to show others what you once sent if you don't send more photos.

If I embarrassed myself, what should I do?

- Move forward. Imagine in your mind another result of the same situation. What should you do, or how could you prepare for the next time?

- Laugh at yourself. Nobody is perfect. Even acclaimed singers, presidents, and many famous people have done things that have put them in a situation that everyone is laughing at. But after all, they are temporary situations, and with the passing of time they remain just another anecdote.

INEVITABLE CHANGES

There is no way to grow without changing.
Lucas Leys, *Different*

Marinette is a normal teenager, she comes from a normal house, has a standard family, and studies in a very normal school, until she meets an old man from whom she receives a *kwami*, a jewel that gives her the power of creation. And it transforms her into a teenage superheroine. Adrien is a boy who comes from a family with a lot of money. The same thing happens to him, only his *kwami* gives him the power of destruction. Together, they are called to fight the dark forces that attack Paris.

Miraculous: The Adventures of Ladybug and Cat Noir is a series set in Paris that has already been seen around the world thanks to Netflix and Disney Channel. It reminds some people of Power Rangers, which was also about an artifact that gave each of the team members special outfits and powers to fight evil.

And yes, you'll probably say that *Miraculous* has a lot of elements of magic and other things, but preteens watch a lot of similar shows so it's better for us to know what they are about. What these two TV shows have in common are the powers that the protagonists receive when activating an X device. They are different, they become warriors, they become heroes. They change, transform their body, their mind, and their abilities. They become brave and confront evil.

We all dream of changing and becoming something better. The wonderful thing about the preteen stage is that this is when it can happen. We can become super special people with the power of the Holy Spirit in us!

AVALANCHE OF IDEAS

Prepare to hand out enough Play-Doh for every participant. At the start of the meeting, give each one a little and ask them to build a shape that represents them in some way, such as an animal that they like, or whatever each one chooses according to their personality and tastes.

When they have finished molding, each one should show the group their creation and explain why they gave it that shape, which will already be interesting. But after everyone has shared, you will give them the challenge.

Now they must work in pairs. (If the number of participants is odd, one of the groups can be of three people). Once they are together, the challenge will be to take both creations and, without changing the initial shape too much, try to create a new shape that includes both figures. At the end, everyone should explain to the group what they invented. Have them name their creation, and have a few laughs as they share what they've designed.

(If your meeting is virtual, ask your kids ahead of time to have some Play-Doh ready. During the meeting, each of you can make one shape and then swap it out for another. The effect will be similar).

Now ask them to look at how much the shapes have changed from their original shape. Most likely they have changed at least a little! With this introduction you can talk to them about the changes that people are undergoing, and how necessary they are. Explain that during this lesson they will be learning about some inevitable changes that they are all going through or will soon go through.

📝 FOUNDATIONS OF THE THEME

Preadolescence is the prelude to puberty, and surely several of the kids in your group, especially the girls, will already be experiencing some of its symptoms. Surely your boys and girls have already heard about the subject, but you can review some general aspects of what puberty is, which usually occurs between the ages of 11 and 13, although in some cases it can start as early as 9.

Depending on the characteristics of the group you are discipling (if you have a mixed group, or if it is only boys or only girls) you can use the strategy that you find most appropriate, such as dividing them between boys and girls for a specific conversation.

Here you will find information for both groups.

THE PHYSICAL APPEARANCE HAS BECOME THE REASON FOR CONCERN IN KIDS GOING THROUGH PUBERTY, SINCE IT MAKES THEM FEEL INSECURE AND DISSATISFIED WITH THEIR IMAGE.

The point is not to inform them about the physical changes, but to give them an overview of the fact that they are beginning to change at an accelerated rate, and that this is good even though they may feel strange in the process. Your essential work as a discipler is to offer them the biblical perspective that other places like school will not give them. Some basic information is always good to share.

The physical appearance has become the reason for concern in kids going through puberty, since all these sudden changes that they experience in their body shape makes them feel insecure and dissatisfied with their image.

"Those physical changes are a whole thing, and I would never minimize them. These are changes visible to everyone, but above all they are visible to the young person who is experiencing them. They live with their physical changes every day and see their whole body like no one else does. In regards to their physical development, kids entering their teens have a stormy combination of hope and

fear. They've been told over and over again what their bodies are supposed to look like, and they live listening to a continuous, incisive internal monologue that repeats: My body isn't right, and things are starting to change."
Mark Oestreicher, *Understanding Your Young Teen.*

PHYSICAL CHANGES IN GIRLS:

Girls experience the following changes to their bodies during puberty: increased height, significant development of bone structure, the appearance of pubic and underarm hair, and the onset of breast growth. Their sexual glands (ovaries) also develop, and this leads to the onset of menarche (first menstruation).

PHYSICAL CHANGES IN BOYS:

Boys, for their part, share with girls the growth in height and the widening of the bones, as well as the appearance of pubic and axillary hair and the development of their genitals. Added to this is an increase in muscle mass, a change in the timbre of the voice, and the appearance of facial hair.

Along with the physical changes there is also the famous explosion of hormones that unleashes a series of perceptions in preteens that were not there before. An interest in romance and curiosity about sexuality arise, and these new sensations generate enormous confusion in the minds of boys and girls. This topic really concerns you as a discipler!

Many parents and leaders are so afraid to address these issues that they turn to the simplest of all attitudes: pretending nothing happens. This leaves preteens totally on their own to deal with an already distressing situation. In addition, you can be sure that if you, from your role, or the parents as the first disciplers of their children, do not give them the adequate information, they will just find misinformation somewhere else. It's the easiest to find!

Can a preteen avoid all of this? No, although they are surely thinking that they did not want to experience so many changes, and that everything was easier when they were children and none of these things mattered. But here they are. These are inevitable changes, and they arrive right during the preteen years!

MANY PARENTS AND LEADERS ARE SO AFRAID TO ADDRESS THESE ISSUES THAT THEY TURN TO THE SIMPLEST OF ALL ATTITUDES: PRETENDING NOTHING HAPPENS.

Good thing they do! The changes at this stage are a precious opportunity to walk towards young adulthood. An occasion to mature and awaken to the purpose for which each one has been designed.

OTHER CHANGES PRETEENS GO THROUGH:

This has been a very general summary about the physical changes that boys and girls experience during this stage, and already in the first lesson we talked about changes in emotions. Now we will talk about the changes in their thoughts, since their way of thinking also changes drastically at this stage.

The childhood brain has been preparing to take these boys and girls into adulthood, and this entails physiological changes, but also changes in their behavior and their way of thinking. Understanding this is key when discipling preteens, as it helps us see things from their perspective. Our job as disciplers will be to accompany them as they progress on this path of becoming adults, while they are learning to be disciples of Christ.

Some things to learn:

- The preteen brain is not yet an adult brain. (That only happens around the age of 25.)

- Preteens will try to take some risks by pushing boundaries and testing what is going on around them. It is the classic game of learning by failing, and although not everyone learns from their mistakes, their brain becomes conditioned to their successes and tries to distinguish what things should be avoided.

- That is very different from how a child thinks! Usually, if you tell a child not to take a certain risk, they will be obedient, or if they are disobedient it will be because they want to get something they really want, not because they are testing their limits. The preteen will feel strong and determined to take that risk even though they have been warned of the danger.

Helpful note: Get Mark Oestreicher's book "Understanding Your Young Teen" at www.e625.com/tienda

Finally, as a discipler you must be clear about these three very important changes that occur during preadolescence:

1. **Responsibility:** This is an age in which they can take on more responsibilities, not the same as those of an adult, but for things that are within their reach. Consider it their spiritual training and their approach to God. Faith is already ceasing to be an inheritance from their parents and is beginning to be a personal decision. That is why your intentional participation at this stage is vital.

2. **Commitment:** They are ready to commit, whether to an idea or to a lifestyle or philosophy of thought. They are already beginning to develop their own criteria. Everything you do at this stage will be key to getting them to commit to Jesus.

3. **Limits and freedom:** Now they realize that they can have more freedom, and they are going to want to take risks that they didn't take before. But just as they want greater freedom, they must be clear about the limits that this freedom implies.

This is a very important topic, and we'll be talking more about limits and freedom in Lesson 10.

📖 FOCUS ON TRUTH

Jesus was also a preteen and experienced changes. And while it is true that there are not many records in Scripture about the stages of Jesus's childhood and adolescence, we do have the following story that tells of an event that happened in the midst of our Lord's preteen years, at just twelve years old.

FAITH IS ALREADY CEASING TO BE AN INHERITANCE FROM THEIR PARENTS AND IS BEGINNING TO BE A PERSONAL DECISON.

You can read the story together with your discipleship group, or ask them to read the passage beforehand:

Every year Jesus' parents went to Jerusalem for the Festival of the Passover. When he was twelve years old, they went up to the festival, according to the custom. After the festival was over, while his parents were returning home, the boy Jesus stayed behind in Jerusalem, but they were unaware of it. Thinking he was in their company, they traveled on for a day. Then they began looking for him among their relatives and friends. When they did not find him, they went back to Jerusalem to look for him. After three days they found him in the temple courts, sitting among the teachers, listening to them and asking them questions. Everyone who heard him was amazed at his understanding and his answers. When his parents saw him, they were astonished. His mother said to him, "Son, why have you treated us like this? Your father and I have been anxiously searching for you."
"Why were you searching for me?" he asked. "Didn't you know I had to be in my Father's house?"
But they did not understand what he was saying to them.
Then he went down to Nazareth with them and was obedient to them. But his mother treasured all these things in her heart. And Jesus grew in wisdom and stature, and in favor with God and man.

Luke 2:41–52

In short, Jesus had gone to celebrate the Passover in Jerusalem together with his parents. He was already twelve years old by then, and when they were returning, in the middle of the caravan of relatives and acquaintances who were traveling together, Jesus's parents lost sight of him. It is believed that perhaps, since the caravan was very large, Jesus' parents may have thought that the young man was walking with a relative or acquaintance, but the truth is that when looking for him, they did not find him.

It can be a bit funny trying to imagine how this happened. Perhaps Mary thought that he was with Joseph, and Joseph thought that he was with Mary, and when they met, they looked at each other and wondered: "Where's Jesus? Wasn't he with you?" "No, he wasn't with me. I thought he was with you!"

This is not how the Bible describes it, but it could have happened that way. What is certain is that when they realized that Jesus was not there, they began to look for him, and it took them three days to find him! This seems too long a time for our modern vision, but consider these details:

- Galilee was about 120 kilometers from Jerusalem.

- The distance had to be covered on foot, and that must have taken them a few days.

- The Passover festival lasted seven days, so they all slept in Jerusalem for a whole week.

- The text says that at the end of the party they returned to their home.

These considerations reveal to us that this trip had already taken them at least two weeks, sleeping in inns or wherever they could find a place, perhaps in portable tents. That Jesus has been missing for three days now sounds more reasonable, although it does not mean that it was less worrisome for his parents!

We read that Jesus was already 12 years old. In the Hebrew culture, from the age of 13, male children were responsible for fulfilling the ritual law without the observation of their parents. That means that they were already responsible for themselves. Jesus was already 12 years old and was about to turn 13. It is reasonable to think that he was trying to take on his role as a male within culture. Of course, what he did was not wise; it was a risk that he took, like those risks that we said that preteens take because they feel that they already have enough maturity and freedom for that.

Some believe that Jesus disobeyed his parents with this act, but there is no evidence that this was the case. Although Jesus's words seem challenging, in reality the way he responded is quite logical: "Why were you searching for me? Didn't you know I had to be in my Father's house?" It was something like saying:

"Dad, mom, you know me. The most logical thing was that I was in the temple, where the teachers who teach about the law of God are. It was not logical that you would look for me elsewhere."

Jesus must have been waiting for his parents to go to the place where they knew he should be. His parents, thinking like parents, surely had a thousand ideas crossing their minds when they saw that he was not in the caravan. Is he lost? Was he hurt? Did someone kidnap him? Those of us who are parents can think of a thousand things that could have happened, but this passage teaches us that we must always look in the most logical place first.

Jesus acted like a real preteen, and no, he never sinned!

What are these intermediate stages between childhood and adulthood, especially the preteen one, for? They help us to mature!

Ask one of your preteens to read this portion of Scripture:

> *When I was a child, I talked like a child, I thought like a child, I reasoned like a child. When I became a man, I put the ways of childhood behind me. For now we see only a reflection as in a mirror; then we shall see face to face. Now I know in part; then I shall know fully, even as I am fully know.*
> **1 Corinthians 13:11–12**

PUBERTY AND THE CHANGES THAT OCCUR DURING THIS STAGE ARE LIKE A MIRROR THAT SHOWS US BLURRY IMAGES OF WHAT WE WILL BE LIKE IN THE FUTURE.

In this section, Paul talks to the Corinthians about how love makes us mature and how we must leave behind some childish attitudes to become adults. He says that what we see today is like a faulty mirror, which makes us see blurry images of what the future will be like. This is also the case with puberty and the changes that occur during this stage: they are like a mirror that shows us blurry images of what we will be like in the future. But we still need to reach maturity as disciples!

Look at this passage together:

Brothers and sisters, stop thinking like children. In regard to evil be infants, but in your thinking be adults.
1 Corinthians 14:20

Here Paul continues to speak to the Corinthian church, this time about the gifts and how they should be used within the meetings. The context was that many were noticing changes in their lives, and experiencing things with God that had not happened before. The gift of tongues was one of those changes. Paul recommends that even though all of this is new and exciting, they should not behave like children, but should learn to mature in their understanding of these things.

INTROSPECTION

In this section you will ask your preteens a question that can have multiple answers:

How is each of you different from when you were a boy or a girl?

Tell them they can think of different categories:

- Physical

- Emotions

- Thoughts

- Sexuality

- Responsibilities

- Attitudes

- Values

Then ask them if these changes have been positive or negative for them. Keep in mind that each one has lived a particular experience that is not necessarily similar to that of the others. Every disciple is different, and you need to see them as a whole, but also individually.

The idea of this exercise is that your preteens identify in which things have changed, and in which aspects they feel different from when they were children. And perhaps, if you manage to win their trust and open their hearts, you will be able to talk about the fears or anguish that these change cause.

DON'T BE AFRAID TO BRING UP THE SUBJECT OF SEXUALITY WITH YOUR PRETEENS. IT IS NOT ONLY TIMELY, BUT ALSO NECESSARY AND URGENT.

Surely they have heard things about some topic surrounding it that they do not dare talk to anyone about, and this may be a good opportunity for you to talk to them about it.

Just in case, we will say it again: Don't be afraid to bring up the topic of sexuality with your preteens. It is not only timely, but also necessary and urgent. Do it calmly and naturally. Do not forget that this generation is different from the previous ones.

 REFLECT ON A CHARACTER

MYSTIQUE

One of the most intriguing X-Men characters is Mystique. She can change shape and become any other person she has seen, so she can take the place of presidents, agents, policemen, or any ordinary citizen. It is her way of camouflaging herself so as not to be found, or to infiltrate anywhere. She imitates not only the appearance of people, but also their voice, size, skin color, etc. She becomes an exact copy of the one she imitates.

Many of the preteens say that it would be a great thing to be able to look like someone else. Being like a chameleon and change appearance all the time. However, in the movie *First Class*, Mystique's character struggles with looking normal, like everyone else, since her true skin is blue and full of scales on her body, with fiery red hair and an appearance that can scare people away. That's why she always changes shape. And perhaps because she feels different, despised, like a freak, she later becomes part of the team of comic book villains.

QUESTIONS FOR THE DISCIPLES:
- Who would you like to look like? Why?

- Surely some things have already begun to change in your body and in your mind. Why do you think these changes are necessary and good?

PAUL

Saul of Tarsus was a scholar of Scripture, and considered the followers of Jesus to be rebellious and heretics for giving any man the title of Son of God. For this reason, he had become one of the biggest persecutors of the first believers in this Messiah, who had come to revolutionize tradition.

In his story, described in the book of Acts, it is said that at a certain moment Saul had a strong supernatural encounter with Jesus. From there, his name changed to Paul, and he became the apostle to the Gentiles, with a deep calling to preach the truth of Jesus Christ to all nations.

If there is someone who knows about changes, it's Paul.

He experienced what it meant to be part of an ancient tradition that demanded strict adherence to certain religious practices, then to renounce all of that and become a defender of the ideals of the Kingdom of God that Jesus had preached. Paul valued his Hebrew lineage as a descendant of the tribe of Benjamin, and his studies as a Pharisee at the feet of Gamaliel, a zealous follower of God's law and blameless in his way of living. However, upon meeting Jesus, his perspective on life changed completely. Paul decided to throw away everything that previously made him feel superior to others, because he understood that the knowledge of Christ invaded him and prompted him to change his way of thinking and acting.

His change of mind was so radical that he later said things like: "Follow my example, as I follow the example of Christ" (1 Corinthians 11:1).

A statement of this nature, acknowledging that now his life would be futile without Jesus, shows that Paul was a different person than before. He had been stripped of the religious Saul that he was before, to become the apostle Paul, a true disciple of Jesus, humble and submissive to the will of God.

QUESTIONS FOR THE DISCIPLES:

- In what way could you identify with Paul's changes?

- Paul's experience is a model for all Christians to follow. In what way can he be a role model for you at this stage of your life?

🖐 MOBILIZE

To close this lesson:

1. Begin by confidently reassuring your preteens that they are growing up and that change is a positive thing even if some parts of the process seem out of place. Don't assume they already know. Help it become crystal clear to them as a result of this lesson.

2. As a next step, bring a female teen and a male teen (ages 16-18) who have a good testimony to your group to share their experiences with changing from preteen to teen, and to encourage preteens to go through this stage with confidence and security. Prepare those teens ahead of time and help them see the importance of inspiring the preteens to feel that it is possible and worthwhile to go through preteen life successfully.

3. Finally, task them with having a conversation about their growth with someone older whom they trust and who exemplifies maturity to them. With this you will be preparing them to be intentional in trying to have good mentors.

LESSON 6

THE FUNDAMENTAL CONNECTION

What comes into our minds when we think about God is the most important thing about us.

A. W. Tozer, *The Knowledge of the Holy*

Have you ever played with Lego? What many years ago was a toy that was hard to find in some cities, today has gigantic theme parks.

Putting together Lego worlds lets you be a creator of sorts. With as many pieces as there are today, Lego creations can become really complex and cool worlds. But of course, none of the Lego people that we include in these creations have the slightest awareness that we are their creators. Similarly, many around us live in the same lack of awareness since there are non-Christians (and self-proclaimed Christians) who live as if their Creator did not exist.

God is the Creator who came to us through Jesus Christ, and ideally each one of us would live connected and close to him. Being disconnected from him not only robs us of the promise of heaven and eternal life, but also makes us unable to experience the joy of living an abundant, purposeful, and transcendent life now.

AVALANCHE OF IDEAS

Get a long enough ball of yarn and some chairs, taking into consideration the number of participants there will be.

The first step will be to circle up, pass the ball of yarn around in a random order, and ask each of the boys and girls to make a big knot or loop with the portion of yarn that they receive as they accept the ball. Ask them to leave a large space of unknotted yarn between one participant and another. Let there be at least two meters of space between people.

Once all the yarn is connected between the participants, the challenge will be that the entire group must travel from one point of the room to another (could be one end of the room to the other) without getting caught in the yarn. Create a difficult pathway that they will have to travel across to get to their destination. A second level is to do this while only walking on chairs. The one who touches the floor will not be able to continue; they will exit the game, and a chair will be removed.

The other rule is that each one must take the knot they made with one of their hands, and they cannot let go of it. It's not enough that you keep holding on to the rope or yarn; you must grab the knot you made on it. Whoever loosens the knot they made must leave, and a chair will also be removed in this case.

As you will soon see, the challenge is gradually getting more complicated. Be rigid in the rules. If someone touches the ground or someone lets go of the knot they made, they must exit the game.

Recommend that they think of a strategy, and that they talk to each other to organize themselves. The less they talk, the harder it will be to finish successfully!

If you wish, you can set a time limit to make it more intense.

OUTCOME:

The most important part of this curious experience is the conclusion.

Gather the group together and ask them to share what they felt while playing the game. Ask them if they were successful or not, and why they think that was. Allow everyone to share their thoughts.

Now it's your time to bring home what just happened.

The yarn represents God. Without Him we cannot live. That is why it was so necessary to be holding it at all times. But the knots were also important, because they represent each person who helps you get closer to God, such as leaders, mentors, earthly parents, spiritual parents, pastors, etc.

The chairs represent the difficulties of the path that one goes through and the decisions that are made in life. Sometimes they make you fall.

WE CANNOT MOVE FORWARD IN LIFE WITHOUT HOLDING HANDS WITH GOD, AND WE CANNOT DO IT WITHOUT THE COMPANY OF PEOPLE WHO HELP US STAY FIRM ON THIS PATH.

If your meeting is virtual, you can give them a challenge. Ask them to find a ball of yarn and when the meeting starts have them go around the house looking for all the members of their family and cover them with the yarn. Do it as a competition, so they can have fun at home. To overcome the challenge, they must share with the group a photo or video of their family tied with the yarn, all together.

You must be able to run the game virtually, setting a time limit for everyone to run quickly to complete the task.

In both cases, this activity makes clear the concept that we cannot move forward in life without holding hands with God, and we cannot do it without the company of people who help us stay firm on this path. Hence the importance of having mentors, leaders, and disciples!

FOUNDATIONS OF THE THEME

Admitting the existence of God is one thing but trusting in him is another. According to Scripture, even the demons believe, although they flee when they hear his name. Therefore, believing is not enough. Trusting in God has more power. It has to do with a relationship that we can nurture. It's the same as what happens with a person you barely know, but as you spend time together, you get to know each other more.

Our faith is incomplete without an intimate relationship with God, and how pre-teens connect with a friend, a leader, or their parents is key to understanding how their connection to God will work.

Ask them to reflect on the following question:

How do you connect with a new friend?

OUR FAITH IS INCOMPLETE WITHOUT AN INTIMATE RELATIONSHIP WITH GOD.

At first, someone tells you about a person, or they introduce you to them. You like that person, and you decide to look for moments to relate more with them. There is still no connection at this stage, you just spend time together, get to know each other more, and start to see what you have in common. If you both continue to encourage the friendship, you will soon find more personal moments, learn to resolve conflicts, and if all that goes well, you will have learned to stay connected with each other. On the other hand, if that connection does not occur well, friendship will remain as something fleeting, like memories of someone you once knew.

To connect with God, we also have to go through some stages, which could be summarized as follows:

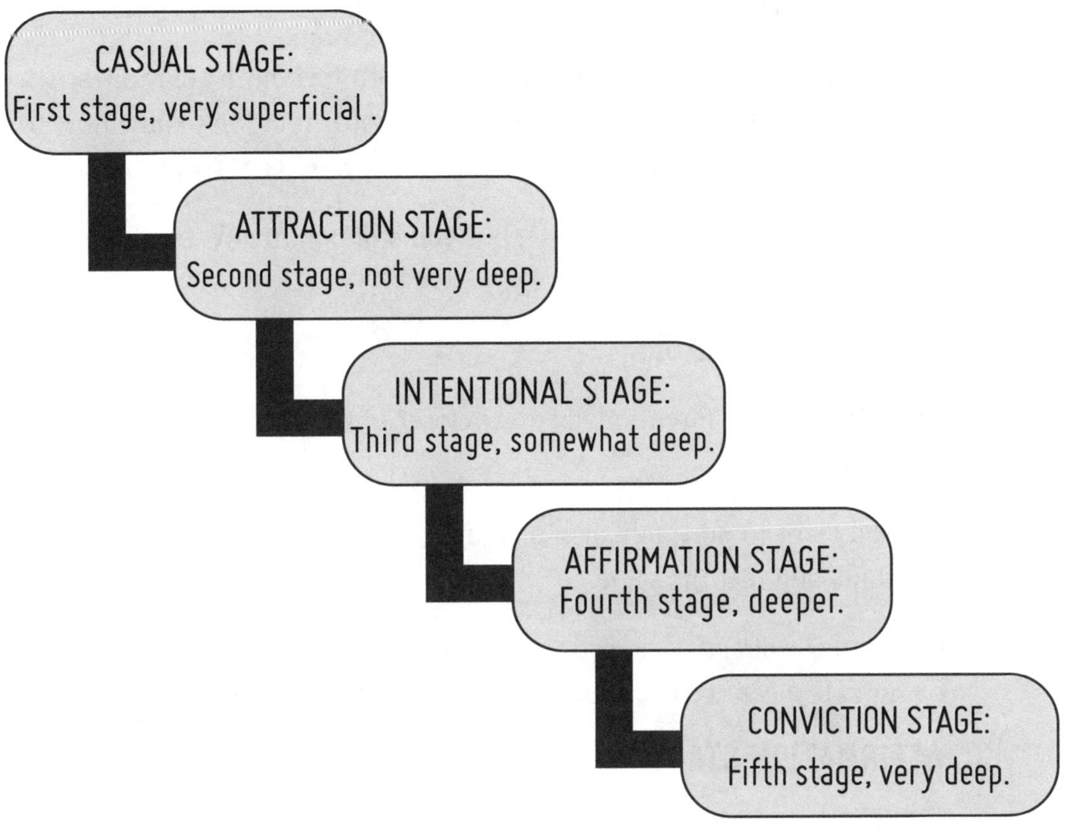

Here are the details of each stage:

1. CASUAL STAGE:

◊ Someone told you about God or introduced you to the gospel.

◊ You still don't understand why those who follow God do what they do.

◊ Your life goes on the same as before, and there is no real connection with God.

2. **ATTRACTION STAGE:**

◊ The gospel caught your attention, and you feel motivated to learn more about that God they are talking about. You don't know how to pray, but you let them pray for you.

◊ You want to change your life, but you still don't know how. There is no real connection with God.

3. **INTENTIONAL STAGE:**

◊ You decide to intentionally draw closer to God to learn more about his Word.

◊ You learn to pray, to worship, and to congregate with others who think and feel the same.

◊ You have already changed some areas that were not good for you. You initiate a connection with God, but you put some conditions on it.

4. **AFFIRMATION STAGE:**

◊ Your relationship with God is affirmed and becomes a genuine faith. You investigate deeply the things of God.

◊ You learn to listen to his voice. Prayer becomes a lifestyle, and you gain new ways of communicating with God.

◊ You put all your effort into changing your life and pleasing God. You are connected with God, and you decide to believe despite not understanding many things.

5. **CONVICTION STAGE:**

◊ There will be nothing that will change your way of thinking. You will follow God to the ends of the earth.

◊ You have a fluid communication with God, you know him through his Word and his voice, and you learn to see God in all things.

◊ You do not live in sin, but you move away from it. Your connection with God runs deep and you motivate others to have a close relationship with God.

📖 FOCUS ON TRUTH

There is no better example in the Bible of connecting with God than that of Jesus. Throughout the Gospels we see him connected with the Father to make the important decisions. From his childhood to the moment of his last breath of natural life, Jesus did everything to please God.

> **THERE IS NO BETTER EXAMPLE IN THE BIBLE OF CONNECTING WITH GOD THAN THAT OF JESUS.**

Where can we observe the connection of Jesus with the Father?

- In his prayers, in which his longing to be alone with the Father was evident.

- In his speeches, he always ended by referring to words that the Creator had inspired the ancient prophets to write.

- In his miracles, which always ended up giving glory to the Father.

- When he talked about everyday things and shared with his disciples, since his words and actions denoted an intimate relationship with God.

- In the fact that there was no sin in him because he always knew that he was set apart for God, which is the true meaning of being holy. That is why Jesus himself asks us to be holy, set apart for God, connected with him, always, in all circumstances, in all calamities, and in all blessings.

Show this sequence to your discipleship group:

When he was a child, at 12 years old...

"Why were you searching for me?" he asked."Didn't you know I had to be in
my Father's house?"
Luke 2:49

...Jesus was certain that the Father wanted him there, doing his Father's work.

At his baptism, before beginning his public ministry...

When all the people were being baptized, Jesus was baptized too. And
as he was praying, heaven was opened and the Holy Spirit descended on
him in bodily form like a dove. And a voice came from heaven: "You are my
Son, whom I love; with you I am well pleased.
Luke 3:21–22

..the Father's words affirmed the connection between them.

Before choosing his disciples...

One of those days Jesus went out to a mountainside to pray, and spent
the night praying to God. When morning came, he called his disciples to
him and chose twelve of them, whom he also designated apostles: Simon
(whom he named Peter), his brother Andrew, James, John, Philip, Bar-
tholomew, Matthew, Thomas, James son of Alphaeus, Simon who was called
the Zealot, Judas son of James, and Judas Iscariot, who became a traitor.
Luke 6:12–16

...Jesus spent the whole night praying.

When he teaches them to pray...

He said to them, "When you pray, say: 'Father, hallowed be your name, your
kingdom come. Give us each day our daily bread. Forgive us our sins, for we
also forgive everyone who sins against us. And lead us not into temptation.
Luke 11:2–4

...the Father was always in his prayers.

At the moment of his death...

Jesus called out with a loud voice, "Father, into your hands I commit my spirit." When he had said this, he breathed his last.

Luke 23:46

... Jesus spoke with certainty that he was about to reunite with the Father.

His way of expressing himself, of addressing the Father, of being one with him, and of asking us to also be one with him, all this makes us see the level of connection that Jesus had with the eternal God. Let's learn from Christ, our greatest example!

 # INTROSPECTION

Put these two lists on a board or piece of paper and ask your preteens to use a line to connect the phrase from the list on the right that best fits with each word on the list on the left.

If you are in a virtual meeting, you can send them a photo of these two lists, and each one can draw on the photo to join the phrases with lines.

Surely they will be able to do it without problems!

MATCH THE ANSWERS	
WITH THIS PERSON:	MY RELATIONSHIP SHOULD BE:
God	Respectful
My parents	Useful
My siblings	Affectionate
My friends	Informative
My teachers	Intimate
My leaders	Trustworthy
My pet	Loyal
My phone	Loving
My computer	Faithful

At the end of the exercise, they will realize that there are some adjectives that can fit in several of the cases, but there are others that definitely do not fit. For example, we do not necessarily see God as a useful or informative connection; we leave that for the phone or the computer. But we can have a trusting or affectionate relationship with God, although ideally it would be intimate.

This activity should produce in the preteens the ability to reflect on their own connection to God. It is likely that some say that they see God only with respect and that their connection does not go further. You should encourage them to improve that connection more and more, since one of the hallmarks of discipleship is growing in our relationship with God!

 REFLECT ON A CHARACTER

LUCY

C. S. Lewis is the author of the seven book series *The Chronicles of Narnia*. In the book entitled *The Lion, the Witch and the Wardrobe* we meet four siblings. The youngest of them is Lucy. Little Lucy is the one who finds the entrance door to the fantastic world of Narnia for the first time, and that is the beginning of a great adventure.

We will talk about Lucy because it is precisely she who is connected for the first time with the world of Narnia, but also because she is the one who is most connected to the lion Aslan, the creator of everything, and ruler of Narnia. Lucy's relationship with Aslan was very special from the beginning, both on the part of the girl (who marveled at the enormity of the majestic lion), and on the part of Aslan (who felt great tenderness and special affection for the innocent Lucy).

In *Prince Caspian*, Lucy appears again, and she is the one who first sees Aslan in the forest. Her faith has not waned, even though she has been away from Narnia for a long time, and none of her siblings have been able to see the lion again. Aslan recognizes that in Lucy and she is a good example of the possibility that we have of being connected with God in an intimate, constant, and permanent way.

QUESTIONS FOR THE DISCIPLES:

- What is Lucy's great virtue?

- How can we develop that faith ourselves?

SAMUEL

The prophet Samuel, writer of two books of the Bible, is considered a servant who was in constant connection with the God. From a very young age he already heard God's voice, and although he did not know who God was or how to distinguish that voice, little by little he learned. Thanks to his sensitivity to hear the voice of God, Samuel was able to follow the instructions that came from him at all times, from things that seemed to be insignificant, to the prophetic acts of greatest relevance to the history of the people of God.

For example, Samuel received direction from God to anoint Saul as Israel's first king, and he also knew when it was time to remove him for his disobedience. He was able to find David to anoint him as Saul's successor even though he was hiding out in the field herding sheep. Even when he was first introduced to all of David's brothers, he knew how to wait for the right one to arrive, the one whom God had chosen.

Samuel witnessed many battles, both victories and defeats, and nothing kept him from the God he had known since childhood. Being connected with God meant for Samuel not only listening to him, but also obeying him, and for this reason he always had the privilege of hearing the audible voice of God that never faded throughout his life.

QUESTIONS FOR THE DISCIPLES:

- How can you know when God is trying to tell you something?

- How can we learn to listen to God like Samuel?

MOBILIZE

Use the chart of the stages in our relationship with God that we saw earlier in this chapter, and develop with your preteens a plan to continue moving forward in this process. The plan may include some general ideas such as the following:

- Turn off all electronic devices, go somewhere where you can be alone, and think about God. Tell them to think about who God is and what God wants for them.

- Go out early in the morning to a high place, such as a mountain, or the roof of a house or building, to watch the sunrise (making sure that it is a safe place). It may be that each one goes on their own, or that they come together to do it as a group.

- Listen to a song one night of the week alone in their rooms, and try to receive what God wants to say to them. You can suggest some songs to them for this.

- Gather for a time of prayer together, in person or virtually, at a different time than your regular meeting.

- Organize a Bible reading challenge during the week. (At the end you can ask them to write, on paper or in a chat, what they feel they have received and heard from God personally.)

Encourage them to do some of these things alone, but also help them organize themselves to do some of them with just three or four close friends. Of course, you can be a part too!

The important thing is that the experience is a new step. This is part of the job of helping a disciple to further their knowledge of God, not just with intellectual knowing, but with relational learning.

LESSON 7

PART OF THE SOLUTION

There are people all around the world who can go their whole lives without knowing the amount of need there really is in this world, or of the importance of what it means to serve others.

Alexa Brown Shannon, *Let's work as a family*

Begin this lesson by asking your preteens what the extraordinary abilities of all the superheroes they know are. Write them down. Be sure to list all the suggestions they come up with. From the classic superheroes of the comics, to the latest movies and TV shows that boys and girls have been able to see. The list will be very long!

You will see that each of these characters stands out for a special ability that has been given to them. Strength, speed, telekinesis, teleportation... They can fly, become invisible, know more about technology than anyone else, or adopt the abilities of an animal.

Then ask them about the powers of the villains, and also make a list of these. You will soon notice that some of these powers are the same as those on the previous list, used for a different purpose. Evil super intelligence, or super speed to steal, or super strength to destroy... Just like the superheroes, only some use their abilities to help people and others only have their own interests in mind.

AVALANCHE OF IDEAS

MY VIDEO

Almost all of today's preteens already have a cell phone or tablet, or have some form of access to video apps, and know how to make a quick video on at least a parent's phone.

The challenge is that you will distribute to each of them functions, abilities, or superpowers, depending on the number of participants you have. To do this you will draw from a hat or have everyone choose a number, and then they will discover what they should do with that number. For example, whoever gets number 5 must make a video as a firefighter, and whoever gets number 12 must make one as a soccer player. So start by making your list of numbered features, and then arrange for each preteen to pick or draw a number so you can spread them out. The features can be professions, sports, or super powers.

Of course, you can simply ask each of them to do something they like and upload it to the network or app they prefer, but with preteens you will see that the most extroverted will be quick to choose and others will not know what to do, so drawing numbers and tasks adds a greater chance for everyone to participate. After having the videos ready, they will watch them together to talk about what their experience was like.

If your meeting is virtual, the activity will work in the same way, except that they must connect through an app or share their videos in a chat so that everyone can see the result.

Close the activity by asking them how they felt and who enjoyed what they got the most.

This type of game can be a great challenge for some, but it will serve to give them impetus to contribute something to the group and will help them reflect on the need to find how to help others.

FOUNDATIONS OF THE THEME

Too many people live without knowing what their gifts, talents, and abilities are, and because of this don't contribute to others the solutions that they could bring. The damage is double because they deprive others of their help and at the same time they do not find the joy of life and end up living lives without purpose. That's not what God wants for anyone, nor what you want for your preteens!

When talking about talents, abilities, and gifts, it is important to differentiate these three words:

- Talents: They are natural capacities with which we are born, and which were developed without much work or effort.

  ◊ Examples: singing, dancing, learning languages, or being naturally athletic

- Abilities: They are skills that we have had to develop over time and with effort and intentionality.

  ◊ Examples: practicing a specific sport, speaking in public, playing an instrument

- Gifts: They are special qualities that God gives us to be more effective in his kingdom. If you want to place yourself in a space within the ministry and work of God, you must find your gifts.

  ◊ Examples: Teaching, words of wisdom, stewardship, evangelism

TALENTS

Talents have to do with our genetic predisposition. We inherit them from the genetic mix of both of our parents, and the preteen years are a fantastic stage to discover talents.

PRETEEN YEARS ARE A FANTASTIC STAGE TO DISCOVER TALENTS.

Sometimes a talent can be hidden for years. We don't know it's there until we try something new, and suddenly people are surprised to see that we have a knack for something we've never focused on before. Other talens come out early because they have to do with something our parents were passionate about. In any case, talents also must be perfected and turned into specific skills, and that is when they also become abilities; before then, they are rather innate.

In regard to talents, there are all kinds of people:

- Those who have one or more talents but never practice them and therefore never reach their potential.

- Those who have a talent and practice it daily, so much so that it becomes their profession or their way of life.

- Those who have a talent and practice it and enjoy it whenever they can, although their profession is something else that is more interesting to them, but that talent will always be there.

- Those who don't even know they have that talent.

- Those who have a talent but because they have other needs have not been able to give it attention.

ABILITIES

Abilities may or may not be based on a talent. For example, we can learn to play the piano very well or play soccer very well because we have learned techniques early on and then we have practiced a lot, but with talent, what we have is an advantage (although it may be used as an excuse for not turning it into the ability it could be). If the talent is present, developing the ability will be easier. If there is no talent, the skill will take more time and effort, but it does not mean that it cannot be achieved. You just have to put a lot of effort into it. Of course, to develop an ability in something, you must like that activity.

Also, in terms of abilities we can distinguish different types of people:

- Those who do not have goals of getting better and therefore remain the same throughout their lives without making efforts to improve.

- Those who like to try various things and know a little about everything, but do not develop any abilities out of fear or shame.

- Those who like one thing so much that they dedicate themselves to it all their lives. Perhaps they did not have the talent and were underestimated for that, but after so much fighting they achieved their desire.

- Those who have a talent and strive to develop their ability by taking advantage of that talent.

One important thing to convey to preteens is that the best way to discover talents and develop abilities is to try. Here are some ideas:

- Sports: It may be that you like a sport and have never played it, or that you already play one regularly. Try other sports, even ones you didn't think you would like. Ask your parents to look up the options, ask your friends about it, or check with a nearby club to see what kinds of classes they offer. You should consider a wide variety:

◊   Swimming or other aquatic sports

◊   Figure skating

◊   Table tennis

◊   And so many others that are almost never considered

- Music: Most preteens and teens show some degree of interest in music. This is very normal, especially in the church, because you always see musicians moving around on stage and music is very emotional. In music there are many areas for involvement:

  ◊   Playing an instrument as a soloist.

  ◊   Playing in a band.

  ◊   Singing.

  ◊   Recording for other singers.

  ◊   Creating music videos.

- Other arts: Music is not the only option. There are many other arts that you can try. Perhaps in some you will discover a gift, or you like it so much that you want to develop the ability. Some possibilities are:

  ◊   Sign up for a dance course.

  ◊   Try drawing or painting.

  ◊   Write a story or poem.

  ◊   Take some pictures (you might fall in love with the ability to capture images!).

  ◊   Join a theater or drama group. Some people love it so much that they never leave!

◊   Make videos (film them and then edit them).

- Vocal abilities: So few know how to speak well in front of others, and this is a talent that can be discovered from an early age. Although you can also develop the ability without having the talent!

    ◊   Think about joining a debate team.

    ◊   You can start leading youth groups, or help your leader lead a class.

- Other activities: Cooking, doing math with numbers and money, fixing things, discovering how gadgets work, remembering anything in detail, the art of imitation, comedy... there are thousands of possibilities out there waiting for you!

FOCUS ON TRUTH

Now let's add to all this with the spiritual gifts...

Here we present four biblical passages that tell us about spiritual gifts. Ask different boys and girls to read the different portions.

- **1 Corinthians 12:4–11**

There are different kinds of gifts, but the same Spirit distributes them. There are different kinds of service, but the same Lord. There are different kinds of working, but in all of them and in everyone it is the same God at work. Now to each one the manifestation of the Spirit is given for the common good. To one there is given through the Spirit a message of wisdom, to another a message of knowledge by means of the same Spirit, to another faith by the same Spirit, to another gifts of healing by that one Spirit, to

another miraculous powers, to another prophecy, to another distinguishing between spirits, to another speaking in different kinds of tongues, and to still another the interpretation of tongues.
All these are the work of one and the same Spirit, and he distributes them to each one, just as he determines.

- **1 Corinthians 14:12**

So it is with you. Since you are eager for gifts of the Spirit, try to excel in those that build up the church.

- **Romans 12:4–8**

For just as each of us has one body with many members, and these members do not all have the same function, so in Christ we, though many, form one body, and each member belongs to all the others.
We have different gifts, according to the grace given to each of us. If your gift is prophesying, then prophesy in accordance with your faith; if it is serving, then serve; if it is teaching, then teach; if it is to encourage, then give encouragement; if it is giving, then give generously; if it is to lead, do it diligently; if it is to show mercy, do it cheerfully.

- **Ephesians 4:11–12**

So Christ himself gave the apostles, the prophets, the evangelists, the pastors and teachers, to equip his people for works of service, so that the body of Christ may be built up.
Depending on the time you have, you can stop at each passage and let the students explain to you what they read in each one.

The important thing is that all these passages tell us about a diversity of gifts with which God has endowed his children to build up the church. Make it clear that:

- The Holy Spirit delivers them, and that is his sovereign will.

- We can ask for gifts to be given to us, but it is still the power of the Holy Spirit to know to whom to give each one.

- The gifts serve to help people mature in the knowledge of Christ.

- There is a variety of gifts because we all need each other.

- We can add desire to the gifts and mix them with our talents for service.

In fact, a good concluding text follows, since it states clearly that whether they are gifts, talents, or abilities, we must use them in the name of the Lord and to bring solutions to other people:

- **Colossians 3:17**

  And whatever you do, whether in word or deed, do it all in the name of the Lord Jesus, giving thanks to God the Father through him.

INTROSPECTION

At e625.com we believe that the new generations are ready for service, because they are not glasses that are filled but fires that are lit. That is why it is vital that with this lesson our preteens internalize the idea that they have talents that they can turn into abilities, and that they can count on God to give them gifts when they use them to serve the church.

Feeling useful is born from helping other people with their needs. That is, to be part of the solution that someone needs. But to do this well it is essential to know ourselves.

Share with your preteens the following questions:

1. What are some of your strengths?

2. What do you think would be a way to discover some of the talents you have?

3. Are there certain skills that family and friends have possibly highlighted about you, such as drawing well, being orderly, speaking clearly, moving with agility, being observant, etc. What are they?

4. What new things, that you have never done before, would you like to try?

5. What makes you hesitate, scares you, or stops you from trying new things?

 REFLECT ON A CHARACTER

SPIDERMAN

A character who needs no introduction is Peter Parker, a young man who, after being bitten by a genetically modified spider, acquires unusual abilities. He is able to climb ceilings and walls, make amazingly long jumps, shoot webs to swing between buildings, sense danger, and lift much more weight than a human could possibly lift.

Before his spider incident, Peter was a very insecure boy. So much so that he was unable to speak in front of Mary Jane, the girl who attracted his attention. He wasn't very good at making friends, and although he seemed to be doing well in his studies, Peter considered himself too clumsy to function well in any area of life.

When this dramatic change happens to Peter Parker, he is confronted with his own reality. What will he do with such powers?

Will he search for his uncle's murderer? Will he dedicate himself to having fun and enjoying life like never before? Can he finally get a girl?

Peter was actually good at other things. He had become a photographer for a living, and had been hired by the best newspaper in town. He was a good student, and in fact he had an A in chemistry and had great scientific skills (he even had his own inventions at home, according to some of the comic book adaptations). However, despite having so many special qualities, Peter had to wait until he had superhuman powers to be convinced that he had something good to offer the world.

Discovering that you are good at something can catapult you to unimaginable places! You just have to manage to see what others probably already see in you. Peter Parker realized that too late.

QUESTIONS FOR THE DISCIPLES:

- What would you do if you had Spiderman's powers?

- What talent do you have that others don't seem to see, and you would like them to notice?

- Is it possible that you have some talent that you do not see but others do? Talk to the adults who know you best and your closest friends, think about their talents and abilities, then tell them what you think they have and ask what they see in you.

JOSEPH

Surely everyone knows the story of Joseph. At just seventeen he had that dream in which he saw that his brothers would bow before him. That would drive anyone crazy! In addition, Joseph was just a boy, but he already had the reputation of being a snitch, because he always went to tell his father about the bad things that his brothers did. It is logical that he has earned their disdain, although perhaps he did not imagine that their anger would reach the point of provoking them to commit that low act of selling him as a slave to some Midianite merchants who passed through the place.

The hardest days for Joseph were in his teens and young adulthood. He spent a lot of time inside cold jails cells. But it was precisely there that he was able to show one of his hidden talents. He did not know that he had the ability to interpret dreams. What he had experienced years before with those dreams where his brothers bowed before him was just a small sample of everything that God could do with Joseph through that gift. Later, it was a dream that freed him from prison to put him in the place of highest authority in Egypt after Pharaoh. And Joseph turned out to be perhaps the best administrator the empire had had in a long time!

Wait... what's this about an administrator? Well, that was another discovery. While he was in prison, Joseph found favor with the jailer, and was put in charge of all the prisoners and all the work that was done there.

Ultimately, his talent for managing resources, and his spiritual gift of interpreting dreams, helped Joseph not only to get out of prison but to save his own people when the time of famine came.

QUESTIONS FOR THE DISCIPLES:

- What relationship can the trials we go through have with the discovery of our talents and abilities?

 # MOBILIZE

To close this lesson, play a series of games in which your preteens can practice different roles. Go to https://e625.com/juegos/ and review which games best suit your situation based on the amount of space and the number of kids you have.

Choose games that have to do with challenges, strategy, where there is a leader, and they must act, sing, speak, or simply give orders and organize. Playing is one of the ways we can best discover talents or natural inclinations!

If you can create a full day or camp full of purposeful games and activities, it will help your boys and girls get to know each other, help you get to know them, and help them develop.

For the week that follows, help them to:

- Identify someone in their family whom they can serve in a concrete way.

- Choose an area of service in the church or in their local community where they can exercise their talent, ability, or gift.

Even if they haven't figured out all their talents and gifts yet, which is normal at this stage, a great way to help them discover their calling and purpose is to create spaces and opportunities for service in the church and the community.

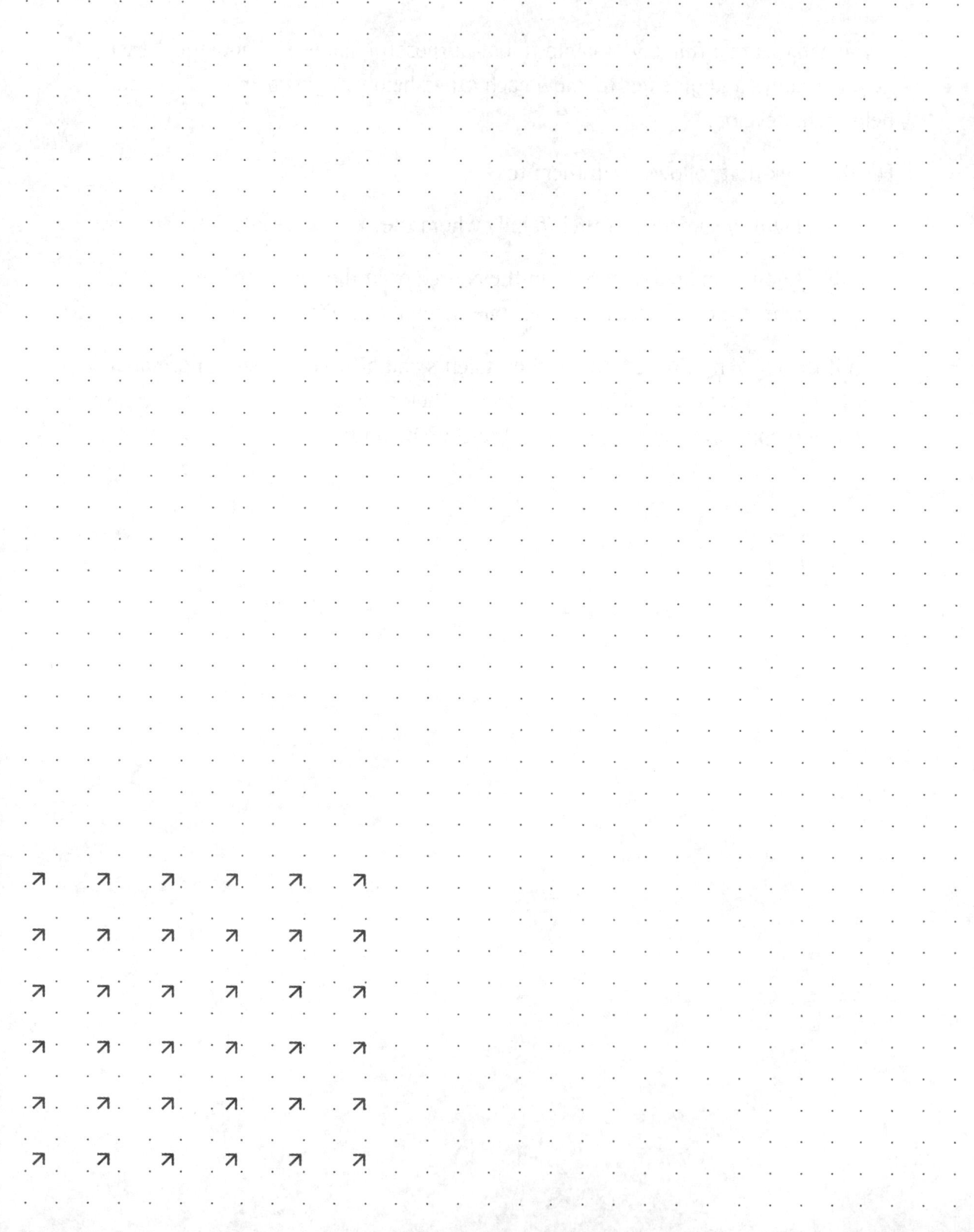

LESSON 8

VALUABLE RELATIONSHIPS

*The story we find in the Bible is that of a being who loves
and continues to love even when it is not reciprocated.*

Itiel Arroyo, *Love is for Brave*

One of the most successful preteen movies of all time is *Stand by Me*, from direc-
tor Rob Reiner. The plot revolves around a group of 12-year-old preteens who
learn that a stranger was accidentally killed near their rural homes and decide to
go see the body. On the way, they meet a bad man in the middle of a dangerous
swamp and the adventure helps them get to know each other better and form
a friendship forever. The film (and the Stephen King story on which it is based)
takes place at a juncture with which we are all intimately familiar, where the last
days of naivety begin to give way to the truths of the adult world. It reflects how
friendships play a fundamental role in the adventure of becoming who we are in
that interesting transition that is the preteen stage.

🧠 AVALANCHE OF IDEAS

You can show a clip from the movie *Stand by Me* and then write the following on
separate pieces of paper:

- Dad

- Mom

- Grandparents

- Older siblings

- Younger siblings

- Aunts and sncles

- Cousins

- Best friend

- The rest of my friends

- Classmates

- Neighbors

- Social media friends

- Friends from church

- Close leaders or mentors

Place all the papers randomly on a table or use masking tape to stick them on a board. If you're in a virtual meeting, have the words appear on the screen. Then ask the group to order these people according to their importance, but to do it as a group, that is, not for each one to say their order, but for them to talk among themselves and argue until there is a consensus, while you watch and listen to them.

Ideally, this activity should take place in a small discipleship group. The fewer people, the better. A good number can be up to eight people. If you have more than that, you could make two groups, preparing twice as many papers.

If they finish early and agree to it, you can change the rules. Tell them to imagine they are children and decide again what order they would assign to each person from that perspective. Finally, have them do the same but this time from the perspective of a person older than them (about 30 years old).

NOW HELP THEM TO CONTINUE REFLECTING:

- What changes occurred when you ranked them as children? As adults?

- At what stage are friends most important and why?

- What relationships are less common but very important?

Note: If your meeting is virtual, randomize that list beforehand so that you can pass the entire random list to the participants. Or you can ask them to have a sheet of paper handy and you read the list of people mixed up. That way, they will receive everything out of order, and they will have to put it in order at home. Then the activity continues as planned.

📝 FOUNDATIONS OF THE THEME

In the preteen stage, boys and girls need to learn to build relationships wisely and know what value they are going to consciously assign to each one.

Every relationship is like a building that you build as tall as you want. However, to continue building, sometimes we have to remove the rubble that has been left as a result of incidents that occurred within that relationship. We all go through conflicts, disappointments, and betrayals, and if we are honest, we are just as responsible for those problems as the others are. The point is that among imperfect people, relationships are never perfect, but that's no excuse for not being intentional about working on them, and the idea is that preteens can start doing just that. We all need support, appreciation, and confidence, and we can all give that to them.

As they enter this stage, preteens discover the power of that innate desire that all human beings have: the desire to be seen and heard, discovered, and affirmed for who they are as individuals. There is an incessant search since the preteen stage, and it revolves around all those points. In that exploration, they are saying various things that point to their inner need and identity.

AMONG IMPERFECT PEOPLE, RELATIONSHIPS ARE NEVER PERFECT, BUT THAT'S NO EXCUSE FOR NOT BEING INTENTIONAL ABOUT WORKING ON THEM.

The inner being of preteens is continually screaming:

I need you to know me and value me!

I need you to listen and understand me!

I need you to know who I am and why I act like this!

I need you not to compare me with others!

I need you to take the time to see my heart!

That's what relationships are all about. In their midst, and through them, preteens are looking for all these things.

Thus, little by little, the preteen is weaving a relational network. We adults, parents, leaders, and disciplers need to be wise enough in the way we help them build their network of relationships, especially teaching them principles so that they themselves can nurture them.

A serious mistake by parents, for example, would be to settle for just supporting the home financially and dedicating the rest of the time to their own affairs, instead of being intentional about establishing a healthy and strong relationship with their children as they grow up. If this is common in childhood, it is very likely that they will lose them when adolescence arrives, and then it will be an uphill battle trying to make up for lost time.

For leaders and disciplers the challenge is similar. If we only focus on holding meetings and don't develop a relationship with our disciples, their spiritual life may revolve around the meeting, but they will end up just meeting an attendance requirement, and creating their real lives with those whom they have more intimate relationships with. If they fail to see us as confidants, advisers, mentors, and older siblings, then they are too far away for us to also be role models and a positive influence in their lives.

If the relationship at home is broken, and the circle of spiritual influence is distant, the greatest inter-action and influence on preteens will be exerted by friends, and they will surely be boys and girls in similar walks of life. The church has long suffered from this evil. Not having been able to deepen the relationship with their younger members, they are more likely to be lost than stand firm in the faith. The same experience happens in the family, where parents don't know what to do with their preteen children and gradually become more and more disconnected from them.

Pastor Héctor Hermosillo writes in the book *Pastorea a tu hijo adolescente* (Pastor Your Adolescent Child):

The best teacher in the world established and modeled himself as what, after much research, educators have recognized as the ideal vehicle to transmit any knowledge: LOVE.

THE BIBLE IS A RELATIONAL BOOK.

📖 FOCUS ON TRUTH

The Bible is a relational book. Read this with your preteens:

One who has unreliable friends soon comes to ruin, but there is a friend who sticks closer than a brother.
Proverbs 18:24

This verse shows us two extremes of what a friendship can be. There are certain friendships that at one point in life can be toxic. For one reason or another they can cause headaches and bad decisions. On the other hand, there are friends we can count on unconditionally; we know that we can trust them because of their fidelity and transparency with us.

This makes us see the importance of choosing our friends well.

Does that mean that if you have toxic friendships you should stay away from those people?

Probably so, at least during a certain stage (like preadolescence) or perhaps at specific time periods (like a school year, or even a camp or event). If friendship with a person is synonymous with bad decisions, then your best decision is to be separate from them.

Look at these other verses:

> *Perfume and incense bring joy to the heart,*
> *and the pleasantness of a friend springs from their heartfelt advice.*
> *Do not forsake your friend or a friend of your family,*
> *and do not go to your relative's house when disaster strikes you—*
> *better a neighbor nearby than a relative far away.*
> **Proverbs 27:9–10**

This passage is powerful because it brings together several notions regarding friendship. First, it describes the personal satisfaction that comes from having a friend you can trust and ask for advice. Then it mentions the urgency of being faithful so as not to abandon a friend, not even our father's friend! This tells us about the deep appreciation that we should give to friendship as well as to our family. Finally, it compares friendship with brotherhood, and touches on the subject of people who are close to us, like a neighbor, who can sometimes become as close as a brother if we know that we can always count on that person. By analyzing all these points, it is easy to understand how important it is for a disciple to choose their friends and the people around them well!

Another passage one talks about fellow soldiers:

> *I long to see you so that I may impart to you some spiritual gift to make*
> *you strong—that is, that you and I may be mutually encouraged by each*
> *other's faith.*
> **Romans 1:11–12**

Here Paul is speaking to the church in Rome, highlighting what a blessing it is to feel encouraged by one another. It is very important to have good friends who accompany us in our process of maturing as disciples. From them we will receive an impartation of the Spirit of God, and we will also feed on what God has spoken to them. We must also reciprocate with them and support them, pray for them, accompany them when they are going through difficult situations, and not leave them alone. They are another important type of friend!

Now let's talk about the relationship with our parents. This relationship is based on honor:

> "Honor your father and mother," and "love your neighbor as yourself."
> **Matthew 19:19**

Jesus, speaking with the rich young man, answers several things regarding the intention of fulfilling the law. Among these things, Jesus mentions two important aspects related to relationships with the people close to us. On the one hand, he talks about honoring parents. This was a principle handed down from generation to generation since ancient times. It was part of their culture, their lifestyle. There was no way to think of living a life that dishonored parents. God's ideal is that we have a very close relationship with them!

On the other hand, Jesus also spoke of loving our neighbor, someone close to us, a friend, and ratified the same condition: we must do it with the same sincerity with which we love ourselves. Jesus's words are powerful, not because they were fancy revelations, but because he spoke truths of life.

How do you receive these passages of Scripture? How could your life change after reading them?

Guide each boy and girl in your group to evaluate their life in the light of God's Word. Ask them to reflect on what a good friend they are, what a good sibling they are, etc.

🔧👤 INTROSPECTION

A good process for establishing healthy relationships revolves around these four ideas:

1. **Zero hypocrisy.** One of the best attributes a person can bring to a healthy relationship is integrity. Integrity is closely related to honesty, openness, the desire to be genuine, and acting without hypocrisy. A relationship that is filled with lies, falsehood, deceit, and suspicion cannot be built in a healthy way.

2. **Show empathy.** This idea of putting yourself in the other's shoes in order to understand them was not invented by any philosopher. God invented it, and it's called mercy. It is the ability to grieve with another in their pain, to help they carry their burdens, to suffer together, and to rejoice in their successes. It's nice to have someone like that walking with us!

3. **Develop familiarity.** How close we consider a person has to do with the time we have invested in being together. Quantity of time and quality of time too. It's not about going to live with someone, or to spend all day at their house and even sleep there (although sometimes it happens!), but it does have to do with taking advantage of the valuable moments that life offers us to share with someone else.

4. **Establish links.** When a relationship is built well, without hypocrisy, showing empathy, and developing familiarity, it is time to establish links. By this we mean finding those things by which you join in a more personal and close way with the other person.

Share these ideas with the group and then the questions stage begins.

That's the best part!

- Which of these principles do your friends already meet?

- Think about relationships you've had in the past that have broken up. Which of these principles were broken?

- Have you valued these principles when choosing friends in the past? Which ones were valued and which ones weren't? How did those relationships turn out?

- What about with your family? Are there strong links? Has hypocrisy crept in? How about empathy and familiarity? How would you describe your relationship with your parents?

 # REFLECT ON A CHARACTER

THE POLINESIOS

In recent years, many YouTubers have emerged who became famous for their videos, and one of them has been the *Polinesios*. Millions of boys and girls from all over the Spanish-speaking world have followed them since they opened their first channel, and don't miss a single video they post week after week. The *Polinesios* have millions and millions of followers on YouTube, and they have earned a very interesting spot of attention.

They are three siblings. Rafael is the oldest, and the leader of the group. Ana Karen, the second, and Lesslie Yahid, the youngest of them. They have a total of five YouTube channels. "Plática Polinesia," the channel of humorous jokes that entertain children and adults. "Los Polinesios," a channel where they talk about their trips and other personal activities. "Extra Polinesios," with fun challenges to laugh for a while. "Muses," where they do beauty, fashion, makeup, cooking, and similar tutorials. And "Juxiis," an interactive channel for gamers, people who love video games. With these channels they have already won several awards, and with their adventures they have definitely conquered the new generations.

They've been at this for a whole decade now, and to achieve something like this, it pays to get along! The Polinesios couldn't have gotten this far if their relationship wasn't a good one. As siblings, we can see that they have a healthy relationship, and with all that they have accomplished, they deserve praise.

QUESTIONS FOR THE DISCIPLES:

- Do you have siblings? How is your relationship with them?

- If you don't have siblings, did you want to have them? Why or why not?

- Would you have liked, or would you like, to have a friendship with your siblings like that of the Polinesios? How do you think they got that?

DAVID AND JONATHAN

The Bible records the friendship between Saul's son Jonathan and David, the king who had been anointed to take the throne shortly. Saul had become uncomfortable with David. When the people acclaimed the young warrior, the king wanted to hang him. Slowly, Saul's discomfort turned into inordinate jealousy, and later he began a terrible persecution against David, whom he thought was a stubborn adversary who wanted to take his throne.

David built a valuable friendship with Saul's son Jonathan. Jonathan became someone very important to him, and that was key at that moment, since the conflict was not temporary but became a kind of civil war, with some supporting David and others (especially the royal army) supporting Saul. By then, Jonathan promised to be David's informant in order to protect him from his father.

What a hard situation! Imagine how strong their friendship was, that Jonathan preferred to turn against his father, the king, to be on the side of his friend. David, in the same way, had to trust Jonathan even though he was the son of his persecutor, and he was able to do so because he trusted the friendship that both had built.

QUESTIONS FOR THE DISCIPLES:

- Do you have friends like this? Would you like to?

- How do you think David and Jonathan came to have such a trusting relationship?

🖐 MOBILIZE

To close out this lesson, go back to the list of relationships and priorities you created at the beginning, as this is a good time to go over an ideal order of priorities. Then guide the students with these questions:

What can you do this week to improve your relationship with your mom and dad?

What can you do this week for some close friends?

Let them brainstorm a few ideas and then give them a card that says, "My commitment for this week is..." and ideally has at least two bullet points for them to write down what they are going to do. The fact that they write the answers to the questions about what they are going to do with their parents and friends this week will be powerful so that good intentions do not remain just intentions, but will cause action.

The following week, don't forget to ask some of them how it went, and encourage whoever tells you a good testimony to share it with everyone so that the lesson doesn't dissipate but rather they see a tangible continuity in their lives.

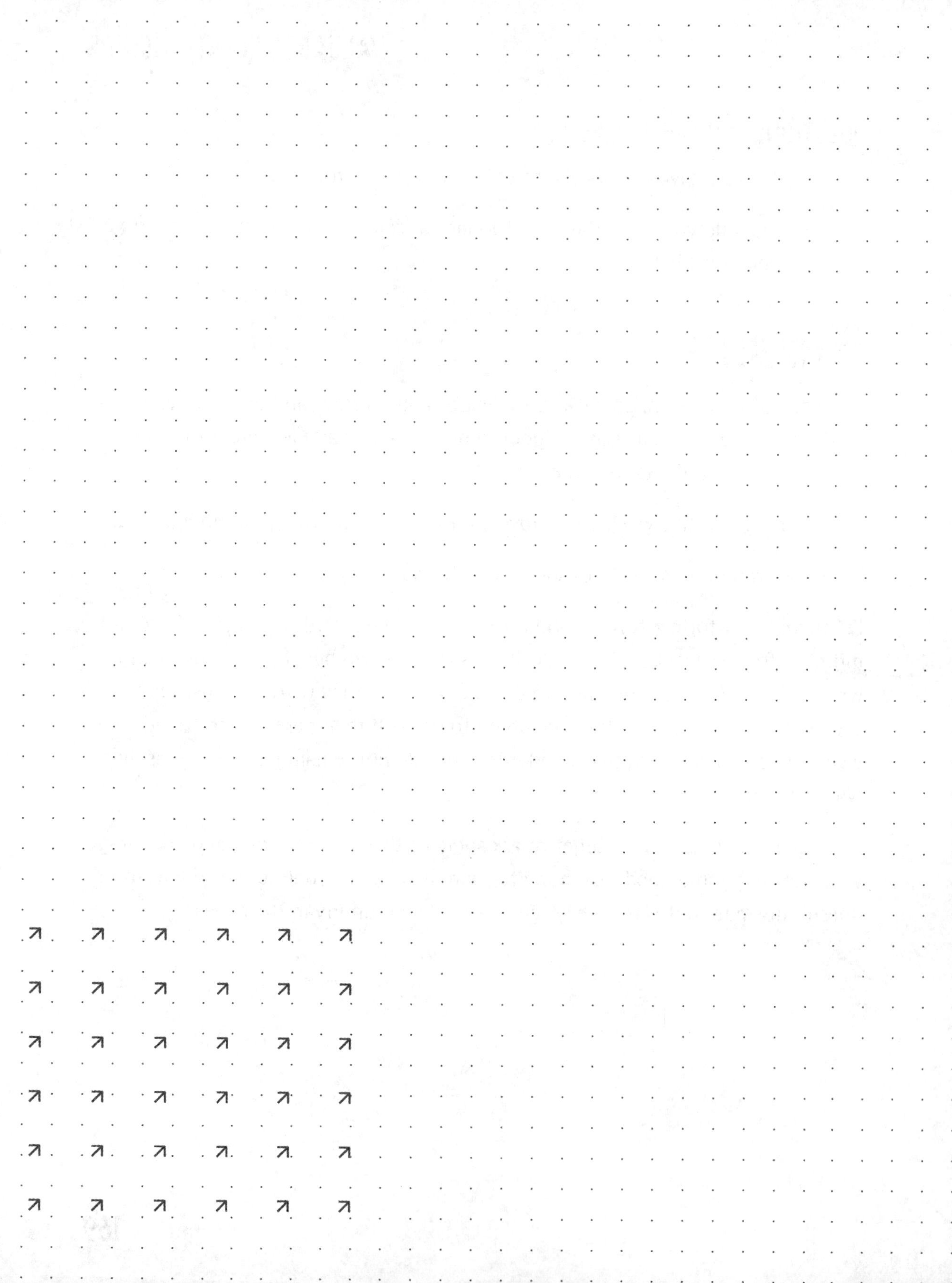

LESSON 9

TRUTH OR DARE

Admitting that we are vulnerable to temptations protects us from them.

Lucas Leys, *Different*

"Truth or Dare" is a game in which the participants choose between honestly answering a question, usually a very personal one, or fulfilling a stipulated challenge at that moment. The game is very popular among teenagers around the world, and some of your preteens may have heard of the game but have never played it yet.

The game is somewhat naive, because no one really knows if the person is telling the truth or not, but what is clear to everyone who has ever played the game is that whether they choose one option or another, there will always be consequences... just as it happens with life decisions.

🧠 AVALANCHE OF IDEAS

You can obviously start this lesson by playing a short version of "Truth or Dare" and/or also by playing this other game that we will call "WARNING!"

INSTRUCTIONS:

Bring blindfolds and choose from your group of disciples two volunteers to blindfold. Plan out an obstacle course for the volunteers to walk through. Do not forget to give precise instructions so that nothing gets out of control.

You are going to divide the group into two: the "Warning" group and the "Go Ahead" group. Now you have "Volunteer 1," "Volunteer 2," the "Warning" group, and the "Go Ahead" group.

The "Warning" group must give warning messages to the volunteer, who must go through a series of previously prepared obstacles. "Don't go that way!" "Wait!" "You'll crash!" are examples of warnings you might give so that the blindfolded volunteer won't trip or hurt themself.

The "Go Ahead" group should give messages with instructions on the direction that the volunteer should take. "Up, down, right, left," "Slow down," "Go down," "Go up," are specific instructions you can give to help the volunteer get to their destination.

Now, let's play!

- **Step 1:** Blindfold "Volunteer 1."

- **Step 2:** You send the "Warning" group to put obstacles in the way. They can be chairs lying down, balls, big or small things, everything they have within reach to prevent the volunteer from reaching their destination.

- **Step 3:** Place the "Warning" group on one side of the path, and the "Go Ahead" group on the other.

- **Step 4:** You instruct "Volunteer 1" to start the path on the count of 3. Give them a time limit of 1 minute to reach the destination.

The volunteer must learn to listen to the voices of those who give him good instructions, but also to listen to those who warn him. It will be a lot of voices at the same time, so it will sound crazy!

Then repeat the activity with "Volunteer 2" making some variations. You can tell them, for example, that now the roles are reversed, and the "Warning" group are now the "Go Ahead" group and vice versa. Or, if you want to make it more interesting, you can ask one of the "Warning" group or the "Go Ahead" group to yell out false instructions to confuse or surprise the volunteer. (But stay close to prevent them from getting hurt by the wrong instructions.) At the end of the activity, don't forget to ask everyone about their experience, including those who gave instructions and alerts, as well as the volunteers. That will enrich the topic we are going to talk about.

> **THE GOSPEL OF THE KINGDOM OF HEAVENS THAT CHRIST PREACHED AND LIVED IS THE EXACT OPPOSITE TO WHAT THE WORLD COMMONLY SEEKS.**

Note: If your meeting is virtual you can help them imagine the situation by explaining the activity and asking them what they think would happen. Or you can directly change the activity by creating a short story where the main character needs to meet certain challenges and the group must decide whether to say: "Warning" or "Go Ahead." Here is an example:

Jorge is going to cross the street. Warning or Go Ahead?

He crossed the street and luckily there was no vehicle passing. But a cyclist is passing very closely. Warning or go ahead?

The cyclist passes by Jorge and only gives him a good scare.

He finds bread on the ground and wants to eat it. Warning or go ahead?

He eats it because he was very hungry. Of course he gets sick...

You can create a whole story and let your preteens decide what to say. The effect will be the same as that of the in-person activity.

📝 FOUNDATIONS OF THE THEME

One of the things that is most needed when working with the new generations is healthy instruction to lead them towards maturity, and if there is something that reflects maturity, it is measuring the consequences of what we do and what we say. There will come a day when your preteens will have to make important decisions that will define their lives, and it is good that they think about the issue to decide correctly, with confidence and security.

For this reason, all of us disciplers who work with this age group are called to find the best ways to offer our preteens all the tools they need to make wise decisions, now and in the future. For this, it is good to analyze the issue of decisions from different perspectives, and here are some.

REGARDING THE BODY:

The most obvious part of our existence is the physical dimension, and starting to make decisions regarding our body is a good starting point, particularly in pre-teens. In order to grow according to our potential it is vital to have good habits for the care of our body.

HEALTHY HABITS:

- **Healthy eating.** Until recently you ate what was given to you, or you ate children's food, but as we grow, we must all learn that it is the responsibility of each person to decide what they eat and what they don't eat. A good diet will prevent diseases and will also give you strength to fulfill God's plans for your life.

- **Staying physically active.** If you already love a sport, great, then you know how rewarding it is to be able to put your body to work. If you don't like sports that much, that's fine, but you should keep in mind that your body needs regular physical activity.

- **Personal Hygiene.** Perhaps until now this was your parents' initiative, but the time has come for it to be yours because hygiene also has consequences. Frequent bathing, brushing teeth, washing hands, and wearing clean clothes are a courtesy not only to others, but also to ourselves.

- **Intentional Rest.** Although each family has its routines, it is good that you know that not having sleep routines harms your functioning. Getting eight hours of sleep is essential for everyone's body, and resisting going to sleep when it's time to do so is childish.

DANGERS FOR OUR BODY:

- **Vices.** With tobacco, alcohol, and other different drugs that exist, it is obvious that they will negatively affect your body and will also harm your mind and your emotions.

- **Unnecessary Risks.** Not dressing warm when it's cold and not drinking enough water are examples of unnecessary risks that have consequences. Not wearing a helmet when necessary in a sport or game, or not wearing a seat belt in the car are all avoidable risks.

REGARDING THE SOUL:

Within the soul we can frame feelings, emotions, will, intelligence, and thoughts. It is necessary to learn to be wise stewards of what God has given us, and that also includes the soul.

HEALTHY HABITS:

- **Cultivate your mind.** Never stop reading, first, the Word of God, but also other types of books. A person who reads is a person who matures and grows.

- **Learn to manage your emotions.** It is good that you can work closely with your discipler to learn good ways to deal with emotional changes and difficult situations.

- **Practice forgiveness.** A person who has not learned to forgive will hurt their heart more and more. Forgiveness is a principle that will help you keep your soul healthy from all bitterness.

- **Love and love again.** Love God above all things, and your neighbor as yourself. There is nothing that can take better care of your soul, your emotions, and your mind than learning the true meaning of loving God and others.

DANGERS FOR OUR SOUL:

- **Early romantic relationships.** God designed everything with his infinite wisdom to happen in the time for which it was designed. For example, you can't run if you haven't learned to walk yet. Romantic relationships were designed for a specific time and age. Don't rush things or put your emotions at risk.

- **Watching inappropriate things.** The internet is full of things that can affect everyone's mind. Parents and disciplers will not be able to be around all the time to tell you what you can see and what you can't, so you must learn to take care of yourself even when no one is watching you.

REGARDING THE SPIRIT:

Last but not least, knowing how to take care of our spirit is crucial for every disciple. From the care of our spirit, a more intimate relationship with the God is born.

HEALTHY HABITS:

- **Pray constantly.** You cannot be a disciple of Jesus without having prayer as a constant habit.

- **Worship at all times.** Not only with music, but with all the arts. Writing, drawing, singing, praying, offering, obeying God... There are many ways to show our worship.

- **Read and study the Word of God.** There is no other kind of food for our spirit, only the Bible. And there is no way to strengthen our faith if we are not in constant contact with the Word of God. That's why we disciplers use the Bible all the time!

- **Be accountable for your actions.** If you have someone to talk to about your struggles it will be easier to handle them, whereas if you choose to walk alone you will have no one to pick you up when you fall.

DANGERS FOR OUR SPIRIT:

- **Getting involved in dark things.** From childhood, the darkness attracts the little ones to lead them to practices contrary to the faith. Be careful with those games that encourage you to open the spiritual dimension, or with people who practice these things.

- **Letting sin cool off your relationship with God.** Scripture says that the Spirit of God grieves within us when we sin. If sin becomes a constant practice, we will increasingly turn off the voice of God in our lives.

📖 FOCUS ON TRUTH

Let's analyze with our disciplers some texts that we need to sow in preteens to create good habits based on the Word of God.

BODY CARE

> *Flee from sexual immorality. All other sins a person commits are outside the body, but whoever sins sexually, sins against their own body. Do you not know that your bodies are temples of the Holy Spirit, who is in you, whom you have received from God? You are not your own; you were bought at a price. Therefore honor God with your bodies.*
>
> **1 Corinthians 6:18–20**

Paul instructs the Corinthian church on many things, and one of them is to beware of sexual immorality. This should not be take lightly and even if the world makes us feel that it is normal, it is not. Too many bad things are involved with sexual immorality: disease, rape and all kinds of abuse, sexual orientation mix-ups, divorces, and much more. And although the sexual area is the main theme in this passage, these verses can also help us establish good parameters in the care of our body in general.

Let's analyze point by point what we can learn:

- **Flee.** Sexual sins affect the body, even if it doesn't seem like it at first glance. That's why you must run away from them to protect yourself not only from sexually transmitted diseases but from many other alterations that can damage your sexual life in the future.

- **The body is a temple.** The Spirit of God dwells in us, that is why we are his temple. And if the Spirit lives in us, the least he asks is that we take care of that body where he is going to live. We cannot invite him to dwell in a pigsty.

- **Our body belongs to God.** The Creator of all has given us a body. It is not a gift; it is a loan. At some point we won't need our bodies any longer, and God will give us new ones. Until that happens, we need to take good care of our bodies. We cannot do what we please, exposing our body to harm because it's not really our body after all; it belongs to God.

- **We have been bought.** Christ bought us through the shedding of his blood. That was the price for freedom, and for our eternity. Therefore, it is necessary to learn to honor God in everything and take care of our body.

SOUL CARE

To delve into what the care of our soul means, let's look at this passage:

> *"The most important one," answered Jesus, "is this: 'Hear, O Israel: The Lord our God, the Lord is one. Love the Lord your God with all your heart and with all your soul and with all your mind and with all your strength.' The second is this: 'Love your neighbor as yourself.' There is no commandment greater than these."*
> **Mark 12:29–31**

Jesus was already used to answering the teachers of the law who asked him questions to try to trip him up. That never happened since Jesus always answered with the truth of God's Word. Let's learn some more things from this text, especially regarding the human soul:

- **Hear, O Israel (Shema Israel).** This is one of the oldest prayers among the Hebrew people. It is a call to listen to the voice of God and his commandments, remembering that he is the only God above all gods. Jesus reminded everyone at that time of this prayer so that they would see that his words came from the Father.

- **Love the Lord your God.** Love has different facets, and Jesus invites us to love God in all of them. If we can hear his voice and obey it, then we truly love him.

- **With all your heart.** To speak of the heart is to refer to the center of life, since it is the organ that pumps the blood so that the body continues to live. But in this portion, it does not refer to the physical heart, but to the interior, to the soul, to the will, to the immaterial portion of our being that allows us to love voluntarily.

- **With all your soul.** That means with all our emotions, with all our passion, with an inner longing to be quenched in the waters that come from God. Our soul will always be thirsty, and the only way to quench it is through him (Psalm 63:1). Without God, the soul of any person will dry up and even if they are alive, that person will feel like they are dead.

- **With all your mind.** Our intellect must also surrender to God. As much as we struggle with the arguments against God, when we have experienced his presence and heard his voice, nothing will convince our minds otherwise. It is necessary to take care of our mind too.

- **With all your strength.** There are physical forces, but there are also the forces of the soul, passion, encouragement, perseverance, and courage. That inner strength that makes us want to continue standing even when our body faints. We must love God with all the strength that has been deposited within us.

SPIRIT CARE

Taking care of our spirit, even though we don't see it, is no less important than taking care of the soul and body. Developing good spiritual habits helps us to keep our spirit in shape and offers us an intimate and deep communion with our beloved Lord.

Take a look at what the word of God says about some of those spiritual habits that we described in the "Foundations of the Theme" section.

- **Prayer**

  Rejoice always, pray continually, give thanks in all circumstances; for this is God's will for you in Christ Jesus.
  1 Thessalonians 5:16–18

  This passage highlights the will of Christ for us, which is that we are praying at all times, giving thanks to God in all circumstances. He also tells us about how prayer helps our souls to rejoice.

  Without prayer, a disciple has a weak spirit and it will be easier for any challenge of life to hit them.

- **Worship**

  Yet a time is coming and has now come when the true worshipers will worship the Father in the Spirit and in truth, for they are the kind of worshipers the Father seeks. God is spirit, and his worshipers must worship in the Spirit and in truth.
  John 4:23–24

  Today there is a shortage of genuine worshipers. We think that those who play an instrument or sing are the worshipers. Actually, a worshiper is known to be led by the Spirit of God. A child of God must be a worshiper in essence, all the time, whether they are sitting on a stage, serving God, or alone at home.

  A true disciple is a fervent worshiper!

- **The Word of God**

  All Scripture is God-breathed and is useful for teaching, rebuking, correcting and training in righteousness, so that the servant of God may be thoroughly equipped for every good work.
  2 Timothy 3:16–17

  God inspired many people to transmit his word and put it in writing. Therefore, the stories in the Bible aren't only beautiful stories to tell. We find God in each portion of Scripture. The Word of God rebukes us, corrects us, guides us towards the best decisions, and enables us to do good.

  A disciple of Jesus should do what he did: read, study, and speak the Word at every opportunity.

- **Accountability**

  Therefore confess your sins to each other and pray for each other so that you may be healed. The prayer of a righteous person is powerful and effective.
  James 5:16

  Accountability to others is important. Those who grow up without having anyone to talk to about their struggles, doubts, internal conflicts, etc., will easily fall into any temptation later on.

  As a disciple of Jesus, you must answer to someone, and when you fall, be sure that person will not condemn you but will lift you up to be better and better.

If you practice all these principles, and many others that you will find in Scripture, you will have a willing and obedient spirit to do God's will, and that will bring great rewards to your life!

⚙ INTROSPECTION

If we could have a measuring device that would help us assess the state of our body, soul, and spirit, what would the results be?

Recall the different aspects studied in this chapter, and then ask your preteens to rate each other. You can tell them to give themselves a rating from 1 to 10 on a piece of paper, or perhaps one by one they can be evaluated by the others. This will depend a lot on whether they know each other well, and on the trust that exists between them. And remember that preteens are sometimes very impulsive with what they say and can be unintentionally mean. Be careful that things don't get out of control so that no one gets hurt.

YOUR BODY

What kind of food do you choose to eat?

What kind of exercises or sports do you usually practice? What other activities that require movement do you like to do?

YOUR SOUL

Are you careful what you watch, listen to, and learn? How does this help you to be a better person?

When you go through emotional situations, such as disagreements, fights, sadness, or euphoria, do you manage to control your emotions so as not to overreact? How do your emotions, when they are out of control, affect the people around you?

What new things are you learning that help you develop new skills? What book are you reading? What topic would you be interested in researching?

YOUR SPIRIT

In what situations do you pray most often?

What Bible reading plan do you have? Do you read alone, or with whom do you read it?

What kind of worship music do you like the most? What songs or artists do you have on your playlists?

Who do you talk with about life's challenges? Who is the person with whom you feel most comfortable to talk about your life?

 REFLECT ON A CHARACTER

SHREK

Surely most of your preteens have at some point seen the DreamWorks movies of this wacky green ogre. Now, let's take a good look at Shrek. He lives in a stinking swamp, with all kinds of disgusting odors. His ears are filled with wax, and he bathes in mud. He has no concern for his physical appearance, and rats can live in his house without any problem.

And what about his emotions?

He is never calm, he gets angry at anything, you will hardly see him happy, and he doesn't know how to deal with sadness. This brings him many problems in his relationships because he doesn't care about others, he despises any character with whom he comes in contact, and he is always fighting with everyone.

When Fiona comes into his life, Shrek wasn't ready for it. How could he win the heart of that maiden with all those unpleasant habits and his irritable manner?

Yes, Shrek is funny. But... is he an example to follow?

QUESTIONS FOR THE DISCIPLES:
- What positive qualities can we see in Shrek?

- What about negative ones?

- Which of these qualities, positive or negative, do you see reflected in any of your actions?

DANIEL

The book of Daniel describes some scenes from the life of this prophet of God, among which surely one of the most remembered, studied, and taught is found in chapter one. There, we read that when the chief of the eunuchs took Daniel and his friends' prisoner by order of King Nebuchadnezzar, he was to give them the king's food and the wine he drank. However, this food had been sacrificed to idols, and for Daniel to eat it was wrong before God. So, he asked the chief eunuch to give him vegetables and water instead. Daniel remained firm in his decision and found that his strength, his intelligence, his courage, and his wisdom did not diminish, but rather increased thanks to the fact that he had remained faithful to God without eating that food that would not have pleased God..

This and other moments in Daniel's life show the extent to which he was willing to stand firm in his convictions no matter what risks he might take. Even King Nebuchadnezzar himself witnessed this, and a few chapters later had to acknowledge that Daniel's Lord was the only true God.

QUESTIONS FOR THE DISCIPLES:

- How do you think you would've acted in Daniel's position?

- When and how have you had to confront others as your were defending your principles and values?

✋ MOBILIZE

Use the evaluations that emerged from the personal reflection section and outline with your boys and girls some individual goals for each one. Make sure that they are achievable goals and that the preteens make a commitment to them so that the principles of caring for their being are always present in their lives.

For each part you can suggest long-, medium-, and short-term goals.

For example, the goals for some of the aspects involved in caring for the body could be:

- **Exercise**

  Long-term goal: Be in good physical condition, healthy, and strong.

  Medium-term goal: Run two miles in ten minutes (remember this is just an example).

  Short-term goal: Run three times a week for 20 minutes.

- **Personal Hygiene**

  Long-term goal: Achieve the habit of constant personal hygiene.

  Medium-term goal: Comply with the ritual of daily personal hygiene without anyone reminding me.

  Short-term goal: Define the best time to shower and post reminders where I can see them. Create a routine that reminds me to clean in the morning when I get up.

- **Nutrition**

  Long-term goal: Eat healthy to keep my body and mind healthy.

  Medium-term goal: Manage to reduce the consumption of foods that I know are harmful, such as sweets, snacks, junk food, sweetened drinks, etc.

Short-term goal: Talk with adults responsible for my diet to help me make better food choices.

As a discipler, take advantage of each of these aspects to create a calendar that will guide you in continuing to address these topics with your preteens in the future. Help them keep their individual goals in mind and thus prevent the enemy from finding a space to bring temptations into their lives.

BOUNDARIES AND FREEDOM

Middle schoolers are more content and confident when they understand the extent of their control.

Mark Oestreicher, *Understanding your Young teen*

Have you ever wondered what God's motivation was for giving us his commandments? Sometimes we put the emphasis on what they are, but we don't think about what motivated them. That is why Jesus argued so often with the teachers of the law of his time, since although they knew the laws by heart, they had lost sight of the reason for them.

Preteens need to know that God-given boundaries are for our protection and are rooted in his love. What according to culture is a limitation, according to God's intention is the key for us to be free from slavery. When today's culture talks about freedom, in most cases what it means is selfishness, and me being able to do whatever I want regardless of the effect it has on other people, or even the long-term effect on my own life.

Preteens are now ready to learn this truth, and that is the subject of this lesson.

AVALANCHE OF IDEAS

Get white masking tape and form a path with it throughout the room where you organize your meetings. Make two parallel lines of tape separated by the width of one foot or approximately 30 cm. The length will depend on the number of participants you have in your discipleship group.

The game is called "The Abyss." Tell them the following story:

This is a narrow path located high up between two mountains. It is a bridge used to cross from one side to the other. On either side of the bridge is a deep abyss whose end is unknown, and this bridge is the only known path to cross to the other side. A group is traveling together and need to cross the bridge, but as they attempt to cross, a guard appears and demands that the group meet certain conditions in order to pass.

You, as a discipler, must choose those conditions. Here are some examples of what you might request:

- Place yourselves in order of height.

- Place everyone by age, or according to the date of birth within the year, starting with those who have a birthday in January.

- Arrange yoursalves in alphabetical order, by first name initial.

To achieve the orders that the guard requests, they must agree, help each other, and participate actively. As the game goes on, you must keep reminding them that there is an abyss on either side. If someone crosses the line marked with tape on the floor, they must leave the group, or they will all start over. Give them a few tries to get them to have fun with the activity, but create the right tensions so that the task isn't easy for them.

You can choose as many different conditions as you want, but don't spend too much time on it because, like any dynamic activity, it can be tedious if you don't stop on time. Our advice is to stop it when you feel it's best and everyone is enjoying it, so they will want to do it again another time.

Note: If your meeting is virtual, ask your boys and girls to do the same at home with all their family members. You can coordinate with the parents in advance so that at the agreed time, and during the first minutes of the discipleship meeting, the whole family can meet in real time and place the adhesive tape on the floor in a room where they have a good amount of space. Playing together will be very good for the disciples, but it will also serve to connect with the parents!

 FOUNDATIONS OF THE THEME

Boundaries are neutral. There are some that are good and others that are unnecessary, and the game of life is to discern which are the ones that God established because those are to protect us.

Some are natural limits, created by God to govern nature itself. That is why it is logical that birds have the ability to fly, and cows do not. Imagine a cow pooping in the air! (You'll blow the minds of your male preteens with this image.)

In addition to limits in nature, God has established moral limits, limits on interpersonal relationships, limits on marriages, limits on sexuality, etc. It's very interesting to discover that these limits have always been present in the history of humanity from the most primitive and pagan societies. Every aspect of life has been designed by God to fit into a space where we can all successfully fulfill our purpose without harming others, and instead be of benefit to others. In this sense, boundaries are rules that God has intentionally placed for every aspect of life to reach its potential of perfect harmony, and every time that the human being has surpassed one of these limits, they have hurt others and themself. Crossing the limits of God

BOUNDARIES ARE RULES THAT GOD HAS INTENTIONALLY PLACED FOR EVERY ASPECT OF LIFE TO REACH ITS POTENTIAL.

always leaves victims. Someone ends up being harmed, offended, discriminated against, or hurt in some way for what this person has done. That is why the limits from God are so valuable.

And what about freedom?

THE RELIGIOUS AND IGNORANT BELIEVE THAT THE LIMITS ARE TO PUT A CAP ON FREEDOM AND NOT TO UNLEASH IT.

Freedom is exactly what God is protecting! A freedom that does not put mine above that of others, nor that of others above mine, so that we can all enjoy it. Imagine how boring a game without limits would be. Does everyone decide where the goal is? It would be ridiculous! However, that is usually the wisdom of this world, which tells you that the rules are unnecessary. The religious and the ignorant believe that the limits are to put a cap on freedom and not to unleash it.

God's idea was not to establish a list of restrictions to have something to bother the human being with. We need to understand and embrace God's limits in our life, so we don't veer off the path toward our eternal destiny. Overstepping the limits of God always generates slavery.

Crossing the limits breaks marriages, families are divided, friendships are lost, and people are hurt. By exceeding the limits, human beings are corrupted and societies are broken, rulers become evil emperors and oppression increases. That is why wars and world conflicts also arise.

In fact, a good definition of "sin" is exceeding the limits set by God.

Putting definitive boundaries in my life makes me:

- Know who I am and how far I can go.

- Think of the other and not just myself.

- Know my responsibilities and enjoy my rights.

- Know how to distinguish between good and bad in order to choose well.

Some problems that show the lack of limits are (adapted from the book *Boundaries* by Henry Cloud and John Townsend):

- Not being able to say no.

- Wanting to please everyone.

- Saying no to good things.

- Not respecting the limits of others.

- Not listening to others when they say no.

- Wanting to control the decisions of others.

- Manipulating situations through emotions.

- Always wanting to get away with everything.

When we examine our own lives and recognize that we still have personal boundaries to work on, we shouldn't procrastinate. It is an urgent need, and paying attention to it will allow us to lead successful lives with people and be at peace with God.

HAVING PROPER BOUNDARIES MEANS NOT GOING BEYOND WHERE GOD HAS TOLD YOU TO GO.

The discipleship project to which Jesus called us in that statement that we know as the Great Commission found in verse 20 of Matthew 28: "Teach them to obey the commandments that I have given you." That is why it is vital that we are clear about this!

Your lifestyle and your decisions will depend a lot on the limits that you decide to respect, prioritizing the effect that your actions may have on others. It is not about repressing yourself, or lacking personal desires. In the things you decide to pursue, there is no limit. You can reach the sky! Having proper boundaries means not going beyond where God has told you to go, especially if the result will harm other people.

That is why houses have boundaries that you cannot exceed. If someone enters your house without your permission, you will tell them that they are on private property. That is why no one can enter a country without having registered at the border before they have crossed its boundary or limit. If you don't register, you will be an illegal person in that place. Likewise, if someone wants to go beyond what they are allowed to go with you physically, you will tell them that they can't. No one can touch another improperly, as it would be exceeding a limit. No one should say hurtful words to another, as that exceeds the limits we have put in place.

Holiness is not reduced to not doing what is wrong, but rather has to do with loving God's limits because they help us to do what is right for others and for ourselves.

📖 FOCUS ON TRUTH

Many uninformed people repeat that God's law is full of prohibitions that make us increasingly unhappy. In fact, many current ideologies and philosophical tendencies talk about how, for us to be happy, we must have fewer controls and more freedom, without realizing that this idea of freedom is often the biggest enemy of human rights.

The mental image of many people, portrayed by religion, is that a holy person is a limited, condemning, white-clad, frowning person. The big problem with this image is that many believe that this is what God wants and, even worse, they think that this is what God is! But that idea is blasphemy because that image doesn't look like Jesus at all.

In John 14:9 he said, "Anyone who has seen me has seen the Father." So, the holy, mature, truly biblical thing to do is to believe that to be holy as God is holy (as we read in 1 Peter 1:16) means to be like Jesus.

The book of Genesis tells us that when God created the human beings, he gave them specific instructions on what to do and what not to do. If only Adam and Eve had listened, we would have a world with greater freedom today. Yes, with true freedom! Unfortunately, they decided to disobey God's instructions and exceed the established limit, and to this day we suffer the consequences.

Let's read chapter 38 of the book of Job. It is really impressive! The text begins like this:

> *Then the Lord spoke to Job out of the storm. He said: "Who is this that obscures my plans with words without knowledge? Brace yourself like a man; I will question you, and you shall answer me.*
> *"Where were you when I laid the earth's foundation? Tell me, if you under-stand. Who marked off its dimensions? Surely you know! Who stretched a measuring line across it? On what were its footings set, or who laid its cornerstone—while the morning stars sang together and all the angels shouted for joy?*
> **Job 38:1–7**

After waiting a while in silence, listening to the complaints and ravings of the pretentious Job, God decides to respond from the whirlwind by letting him know the difference between a mere mortal and the Creator of the universe, the one who laid the foundations of the Earth and calculated its dimensions, the one who gave it sustenance in endless space, while all the angels looked at his work in ecstasy.

Keep reading:

> *Who shut up the sea behind doors when it burst forth from the womb, when I made the clouds its garment and wrapped it in thick*

darkness, when I fixed limits for it and set its doors and bars in place, when I said, "This far you may come and no farther; here is where your proud waves halt"?
Job 38:8–11

It was God who set limits to the seas that grew proud from the depths and enclosed them by establishing borders. And so he did with everything in creation, including the human being. It's because limits are healthy, and they bring us freedom. Without limits we live at the expense of our own selfishness and evil.

What did Job learn?

- That God is sovereign and infinitely wise.

- That without its limits the world is chaos.

- That God gave us freedom to govern the Earth, but not to exceed its limits.

- That sometimes we know so little about God, or are so arrogant, that we decide to defy his advice, but this always ends badly.

We see all this later, in chapter 42. There, Job reflects and summarizes what he has learned:

Then Job replied to the Lord: "I know that you can do all things; no purpose of yours can be thwarted. You asked, 'Who is this that obscures my plans without knowledge?' Surely I spoke of things I did not understand, things too wonderful for me to know.
"You said, 'Listen now, and I will speak; I will question you, and you shall answer me.' My ears had heard of you but now my eyes have seen you. Therefore I despise myself and repent in dust and ashes."
Job 42:1–6

Job understood that everything he had said before as he was judging God was a huge mistake on his part. And finally, he understood that the limits that God established were the best for the human being. He says, "I had heard of you, but now my eyes have seen you." Job knew God more deeply through everything that happened to him. His eyes were opened, and he could see the magnificence of the Creator who set limits to the seas and designed everything with perfect intelligence. This revelation would forever change his destiny, just as it can change ours when we finally understand these things.

INTROSPECTION

What is the law of gravity and the rotation of our planet on its own axis for?

The short answer is: for life on Earth to work.

Allow the group to consider various situations where nature has gotten out of hand. You can give them some ideas such as tsunamis, earthquakes, tidal waves, fires, floods, droughts, etc.

And what happens when human beings exceed their boundaries?

Here you can discuss various types of boundaries that every preteens should consider.

What kind of boundaries should I put on...

- ...the way I dress?

- ...the way I speak?

- ...the things I see on the internet?

- ...the time I spend playing video games?

- ... the way I respect and honor my parents?

- ... what I eat?

You can add as many ideas to this list as you like, taking into account the particular needs of your group of disciples and what you have seen in them.

 REFLECT ON A CHARACTER

FLASH

Barry Allen was an ordinary young man until the explosion of a particle accelerator gives him the ability to be faster than light or sound. From there he begins his adventures facing other humans affected by the same explosion but who have become evil.

This character taken from the comics offers us a good example of what boundaries mean. In his fight against metahumans, Barry Allen makes use of another of his abilities, which is to travel through time. That wasn't his plan, but those trips to the past and future open dimensional portals creating all sorts of rifts and triggering situations that Barry, in his Flash persona, will have to deal with.

It's not his fault, since his intentions were always good, but along the way he made decisions that made everything worse. That is why human beings do not have the capacity to go so fast or to move in time. Those are boundaries set by God, and they are good!

QUESTIONS FOR THE DISCIPLES:

- Since we already talked in another lesson about what supernatural powers you would like to have, what if instead of thinking about speed we think about other powers such as opening dimensional portals to "see the other person's memories"? Or "know if they are lying or telling the truth," or "speak all the languages of the world"?

- How would you use those powers?

- How far could you use them freely and where would your limits be?

DAVID

David's story is one of the most famous and well known of all time. In fact, we already mentioned it in an earlier chapter when we were talking about friendship. The Bible describes David's most glorious moments and his darkest as well. But what can we learn from David about limits?

A lot!

His story is told in the first book of the prophet Samuel, and you can really learn a lot from him if you read Scripture little by little. At the time when Goliath was tormenting King Saul's army, David was only a teenager. Saul wanted to offer him his armor and sword to go face the giant, but David did not accept. He knew his limitations as a warrior, since he was young. Goliath would not end up being faced by David, but by God himself, thanks to the fact that David decided not to show off but to let God work.

Later, when Saul was jealous of David and was persecuting him, David had opportunities to stop Saul and even kill him, but he didn't because Saul was king. David never exceeded that limit, choosing to honor Saul's authority even though he had already been anointed to be his replacement. Not exceeding that limit out of respect for God and the king earned David the favor of all those who followed him.

On the other hand, the story with Bathsheba was one of those in which David exceeded his limits. Bathsheba was another man's wife, and David wanted her for himself. That's why he lied, committed adultery, and became proud and blind. But the consequences of crossing the limits that God had set did not end there! David ordered the killing of Bathsheba's husband after Bathsheba had become pregnant.

He married her, but that son died shortly after birth. And finally, God did not allow David to build the temple that he had dreamed of for so long.

Crossing boundaries is never a good idea!

QUESTIONS FOR THE DISCIPLES:

- Why can we trust God's limits?

- How can we help each other not to cross them?

MOBILIZE

Talking about limits with our preteens cannot be limited to abstract or general statements. We must concretely help them establish positive boundaries in their lives to increase their freedom.

According to Henry Cloud and John Townsend, writers of the book *Boundaries*, there are several parameters that we should consider when setting concrete limits in our lives.

- **In our words...**

  How can you improve your way of speaking?

- **With our time...**

  What distractions make you waste time?

- **In our emotions...**

  What things mess with your emotions and make you lose control?

- **With people...**

  What people around you are toxic, or distract you from doing good and lead you to make bad decisions.

- **In the order...**

  What area of your life can you improve and how could you achieve it?

To close the lesson, you can ask these general questions so that they have an opportunity to share some of their answers. Make it very clear to them that the exercise of answering the questions is not to add guilt but to begin to live in personal freedom beyond the limits imposed by their parents.

The limits that God put in place for us are like guardrails that protect us from colliding with others and from experiencing accidents ourselves.

The discipleship project is just beginning for your preteens. Now they should discover a personal criterion to take care of their freedom and that of others. It's fundamental for them to become everything that God wants them to be and become more and more like Jesus.

BIBLIOGRAPHY

- **Arroyo, Itiel.** *La prueba del amor.* Dallas, Texas. Editorial E625. 2018.

- **Brown, Rich/Shannon, Elisa.** *Trabajemos en familia.* Dallas, Texas. Editorial E625. 2019.

- **Colbert, Don.** *Emociones que matan.* Nashville, Tennessee. Editorial Betania, Grupo Nelson. 2006.

- **Hermosillo, Héctor.** *Pastorea a tu hijo adolescente.* Dallas, Texas. Editorial E625. 2018.

- **Lewis, C.S.** *Las Crónicas de Narnia. El león, la bruja y el ropero.* Bogotá, Colombia. Editorial Planeta Colombiana S.A. 2008.

- **Leys, Lucas.** *Diferente.* Miami, Florida. Editorial Vida. 2015.

- **Leys, Lucas.** *Liderazgo Generacional.* Dallas, Texas. Editorial e625. 2017.

- **Leys, Lucas.** *Stamina.* Dallas, Texas. Editorial e625. 2019.

- **Leys, Lucas/Burns, Jim.** *El código de la pureza.* Miami, Florida. Editorial Vida. 2012.

- **McDowell, Josh.** *Relaciones.* El Paso, Texas. Editorial Mundo Hispano. 2007.

- **McDowell, Josh.** *La generación desconectada.* El Paso, Texas. Editorial Mundo Hispano. 2003.

- **McDowell, Josh.** *La verdad desnuda.* Weston, Florida. Editorial Patmos. 2011.

- **Obando, Esteban/Lacota, Karen/Intrieri, Adrián.** *Manual de consejería para el trabajo con adolescentes.* Dallas, Texas. Editorial e625. 2018.

- **Oestreicher, Mark.** *Entiende a tu preadolescente.* Dallas, Texas. Editorial E625. 2016.

- **Sampedro, Alex.** *Artesano.* Dallas, Texas. Editorial e625. 2018.

- **Scataglini, Sergio.** *Las doce transgresiones.* Lake Mary, Florida. Editorial Casa Creación. 2011.

- **Townsend, John.** *Límites con los adolescentes.* Miami, Florida. Editorial Vida. 2006.

- **Ortiz, Félix.** *Cada joven necesita un mentor.* Dallas, Texas. Editorial e625. 2017.

- **Ortiz, Félix.** *Valores.* Dallas, Texas. Editorial e625. 2019.

SOME QUESTIONS YOU MAY ASK:

WHO IS BEHIND THIS BOOK?

Especialidades 625 is a team of pastors and servants from different countries, different denominations, different church sizes and styles, that love Christ and the new generations.

e625.com

WHAT IS E625.COM ABOUT?

Our passion is to help families and churches in Latin America to find good materials and resources for discipleship of the new generations and that is why our website serves parents, pastors, teachers, and leaders in general 365 days a year through www.e625.com with free resources.

ZONA DE CONTENIDO
PREMIUM

WHAT IS PREMIUM SERVICE?

In addition to reflections and free short materials, we have a service of lessons, series, research, online books, and audiovisual resources to facilitate your task. Your church can access this service per congregation with a monthly subscription that allows all the leaders of a local church to download materials to share as a team and make the necessary copies that they find relevant for the different activities of the congregation or their families.

CAN I EQUIP MYSELF WITH YOUR HELP?

It would be a privilege to help you and with that objective we have our events and our possibilities of formal education. Visit www.e625.com/Eventos to find out about our seminars and go www.institutoE625.com to learn about the online courses offered by Instituto e6.25

DO YOU WANT CONTINUOUS UPDATES?

Register right now for e625.com updates depending on your field of work: children, preteens, teens, young adults.

LET'S LEARN TOGETHER!

e625.com   /e625com

Downloads
suscriptions
Free
Resources
Store
Chat
Magazine
FAMILIAS SANAS + IGLESIAS FUERTES
PASTORES
NIÑOS
INSTITUTO
e625
Online Education
www.institutoe625.com
Books
Seminars
Events
e625.com